AMERICAN GARDEN DESIGN

AMERICAN GARDEN DESIGN

An Anthology of Ideas that Shaped Our Landscape

Edited by
DIANE KOSTIAL MCGUIRE

A **Horticulture** Book

MACMILLAN
U.S.A.

MACMILLAN
A Prentice Hall/Macmillan Company
15 Columbus Circle
New York, New York 10023

A **Horticulture** Book
An Affiliate of *Horticulture,* The Magazine of American Gardening

Library of Congress Cataloging-in-Publication Data

American garden design : an anthology of ideas that shaped our landscape / edited
  by Diane Kostial McGuire.
    p. cm.
  "A Horticulture book."
  Includes bibliographical references and index.
  ISBN 0-671-79921-5
  1. Gardens—Design. 2. Gardens—United States—Design.
I. McGuire, Diane Kostial.
SB472.45.A54 1994
712—dc20   94-578
                                                  CIP

ISBN: 0-671-79921-5

Designed by Richard Oriolo

Manufactured in the United States of America

10 9 8 7 6 5 4 3 2 1

First Edition

ACKNOWLEDGMENTS

In addition to Thomas C. Cooper, Editor of *Horticulture*, I am indebted to Rebecca W. Atwater, Executive Editor, Macmillan; Virginia Lopez Beggs, Author, Landscape Historian; Helaine Kaplan Prentice, Director Landmarks Commission, Oakland, California; Walter Punch, Head Librarian, Massachusetts Horticultural Society; Rachel Simon, Associate Editor, Macmillan; Nan Sinton, *Horticulture;* Judith B. Tankard, Author, Landscape Historian; John Havens Thornton, Artist, Photographer; George Waters, Editor, *Pacific Horticulture;* Barbara H. Watson, McGuire-Watson Landscape Architects; and my sister Shelby and brother-in-law Richard Guelick III; and the following institutions: The Library of the Boston Athenaeum; The Library of the College of Environmental Design, University of California, Berkeley; The Garden Library at Dumbarton Oaks, Washington, D.C.; The Library of the Graduate School of Design, Harvard University, Cambridge; The Library of the Massachusetts Horticultural Society, Boston; The Pierce Library, Little Compton, Rhode Island, and the Telegraph Office in Taxco, Mexico, for their contributions to this effort.

CONTENTS

Contents

PREFACE

I have been carrying the idea of a popular design anthology in my mind for many years, an idea not fully formed, of course, but more than a mere idea. The catalyst provided by Tom Cooper and *Horticulture* magazine has enabled me finally to cast my eye over two centuries of writing in landscape gardening, and to see the whole as a constellation of stars, which illuminates the way, both for the practitioner of landscape architecture and for the general gardening public.

Initially, I established four selection criteria, which have served me well, because it was only by these means that I was able to maintain a certain intensity of focus; otherwise the subject matter would have been too diverse.

First, the writer's work must be American, the writer not necessarily born in America or even an American citizen, but one who lived primarily in the United States and practiced and wrote in this country. Therefore, the well-known English designer and writer, Gertrude Jekyll, could not be included, although she did some garden designing in the United States, nor could the American writer-practitioner, Rose Standish Nichols, who wrote primarily about issues of design in other countries such as Italy and Portugal. On the other hand, a designer such as John McLaren, best known for his design of Golden Gate Park in San Francisco, who was born in Scotland and trained at The Royal Botanic Garden in Edinburgh, is included because of his magnificent work in California and because of the intelligence and clarity expressed in his writing and its validity for the American homeowner, then and now.

The second criterion, and perhaps the most important,

is that the author also be a designer, that is, a landscape gardener or landscape architect. I strongly believe that the practicing designer has an understanding of spatial relationships that give his or her writing greater authenticity than that of nondesigner writers.

All garden designers, no matter how poetic their soaring fancies may be, are also by nature practical. Translating the plan successfully from the surface of the paper to the surface of the ground requires determination, patience, and communication with those who are actually constructing the work. Therefore, much of this writing is of a practical nature, a distillation of years on the sites "listening," as Beatrix Farrand said she did, and as Robert Zion does, gaining great arboricultural expertise, in order to translate this vision into reality. This literature of design was for the most part written during and after the time the designer had worked on a considerable number of projects so it represents experience as well as ideology.

In some cases, such as Thomas Jefferson's, work in garden design was incidental to other design work he did, but it was nevertheless important. For many of the women, such as Grace Tabor and Alice Morse Earle, their writings are better known than their design work, and the reverse is true for certain of the men such as Frederick Law Olmsted and Thomas Church.

Because of this criterion that the author must be a designer, I have not included many excellent authors who have written about design issues specifically American in character—writers such as Ada Louise Huxtable, John B. Jackson, Jane Holtz Kay, Albert Fein, and John S. Stilgoe.

The third requirement is that the excerpt be from a book primarily intended to communicate with the general gardening public. There are no excerpts from private letters and no articles from magazines or scholarly journals. Many landscape designers have written, particularly in the past twenty years, most interesting and provocative statements intended to encourage professional dialogue. These articles, which have appeared in professional journals and chapbooks, discuss issues that usually go beyond garden design toward more abstract ideas that have farther-reaching implications. This is especially true of the writings of Robert Smithson, which are of particular value in illuminating the geologic aspects of landscape art. The titles of selected works for further reading are included in the bibliography.

The fourth and most difficult criterion has been my wish to keep a balance between the number of entries by men and women. There are eleven women and twelve men represented. Historically, because of social attitudes that prevented women from preparing for and entering professions, there have been many more landscape designers who are men than women. The American Society of Landscape Architects was formed in 1899, and shortly afterwards began to publish "Landscape Architecture Quarterly." For the first twenty years, the articles in the Quarterly were written almost solely by men. During this same period of time, however, the women's magazines, such as *House Beautiful*, became very powerful and offered a forum for women writers on garden design. The social transformations that characterized this era allowed women to break many earlier bonds and become true professionals, although the scale of work that they were encouraged to undertake was somewhat limited. Whereas men, in addition to their work on residential gardens, carried out larger-scale projects, particularly in park and recreation design, women's design work was restricted primarily to garden design and to smaller-scale public projects. Nevertheless, this new-found freedom is illustrated by the vast outpouring of books written by women on garden design in the first half of this century.

At the present time this imbalance is being corrected, and within some of the design schools female students outnumber male students. Therefore, in order to achieve this balance, many men who would be obvious choices, such as Jens Jensen, Ralph Cornell, and Henry Arnold, have not been included, and some women, who are certainly not household names, have been included. This creates an imbalance of another sort, but in the end the writing itself balances the scales.

Some books I simply could not bring myself to include. I decided against *New American Farmer* (1828), for example, whose author, Thomas G. Fessenden, wrote:

> The cultivation of flowers is an appropriate amusement for young ladies. It teaches neatness, cultivates a correct taste, and furnishes the mind with many pleasing ideas.

The desire to educate, indeed the necessity to educate, has been felt by many designers to be an essential corollary of their design practice. Exemplary, in this way, was Fletcher Steele, who in addition to his practice, undertook many speaking engagements and wrote numerous articles for professional and popular journals, with the intention of educating professionals and laymen alike about various aspects of landscape design. Many of the women practitioners, such as Ruth Bramley Dean and Marion Cruger Coffin, and a considerable number of men including James Rose, Garrett Eckbo, and Lawrence Halprin, have seriously undertaken communication with a wider public as an extension of their design practices. In a similar manner, the publication of *American Garden Design* follows in this tradition. Their writings illuminate with great precision the importance of design in the creation of gardens and the many enduring principles of good design.

DIANE KOSTIAL MCGUIRE
LANDSCAPE ARCHITECT
BOSTON, MASSACHUSETTS
1994

A NOTE FROM THE EDITOR

The written material included herein is from the eighteenth, nineteenth, and twentieth centuries. Each entry represents its time, and as such, possesses distinctive characteristics, which differentiate it from all other entries and from all other times. I believe it is essential to preserve the character and uniqueness of each of these writings, and therefore, they appear in their original form. In many instances, there have been changes over time in the botanical nomenclature. The nomenclature is printed here as it originally appeared.

THOMAS JEFFERSON
(1743–1826)

*One of the reasons Thomas Jefferson seems, for all his
brilliance, to be more accessible than many presidents after
him, was his passion for gardening and for the visual
improvement and ornamentation of his properties.
Throughout his life he observed gardens, made sketches,
developed innumerable plans and oversaw their
implementation. At Monticello he carried out the idea of the
ornamental farm, which he designed in the romantic,
informal, flowing style with emphasis on naturalism and
with the use of plants both native and exotic. In all, after
leaving the presidency he wrote, "But though I am an old
man, I am but a young gardener."*

THOMAS JEFFERSON'S GARDEN BOOK
1766–1824

With Relevant Extracts From His Other Writings

A Tour to Some of the Gardens of England

(Memorandum made on a tour to some of the gardens in England, described by Whateley in his book on Gardening.)

While his descriptions, in point of style, are models of perfect elegance and classical correctness, they are as remarkable for their exactness. I always walked over the gardens with his book in my hand, examined with attention the particular spots he described, found them so justly characterized by him as to be easily recognized, and saw with wonder, that his fine imagination had never been able to seduce him from the truth. My inquiries were directed chiefly to such practical things as might enable me to estimate the expense of making and maintaining a garden in that style. My journey was in the months of March and April, 1786.

Chiswick.—Belongs to Duke of Devonshire. A garden about six acres;—the octagonal dome has an ill effect, both within and without: the garden shows still too much of art. An obelisk of very ill effect; another in the middle of a pond useless.

. . .

Hampton-Court.—Old fashioned. Clipt yews grown wild.

. . .

Source: Philadelphia: The American Philosophical Society, 1944.

Twickenham.—Pope's original garden, three and a half acres. Sir. Wm. Stanhope added one and a half acres. This is a long narrow slip, grass and trees in the middle, walk all around. Now Sir Wellbore Ellis's. Obelisk at bottom of Pope's garden, as monument to his mother. Inscription, "Ah! Editha, matrum optima, mulierum amantissima, Vale." The house about thirty yards from the Thames: the ground shelves gently to the water side; on the back of the house passes the street, and beyond that the garden. The grotto is under the street, and goes out level to the water. In the centre of the garden a mound with a spiral walk round it. A rookery.

. . .

Esher-Place.—The house in a bottom near the river; on the other side the ground rises pretty much. The road by which we come to the house forms a dividing line in the middle of the front; on the right are heights, rising one beyond and above another, with clumps of trees; on the farthest a temple. A hollow filled up with a clump of trees, the tallest in the bottom, so that the top is quite flat. On the left the ground descends. Clumps of trees, the clumps on each hand balance finely—a most lovely mixture of concave and convex. The garden is of about forty-five acres, besides the park which joins. Belongs to Lady Frances Pelham.

. . .

Claremont.—Lord Clive's. Nothing remarkable.

. . .

Paynshill.—Mr. Hopkins. Three hundred and twenty-three acres, garden and park all in one. Well described by Whately. Grotto said to have cost £7,000. Whately says one of the bridges is of stone, but both now are of wood, the lower sixty feet high: there is too much evergreen. The dwelling-house built by Hopkins, ill-situated: he has not been there in five years. He lived there four years while building the present house. It is not finished; its architecture is incorrect. A Doric temple, beautiful.

. . .

Woburn.—Belongs to Lord Peters. Lord Loughborough is the present tenant for two lives. Four people to the farm, four to the pleasure garden, four to the kitchen garden. All are intermixed, the pleasure garden being merely a highly-ornamented walk through and round the divisions of the farm and kitchen garden.

. . .

Caversham.—Sold by Lord Cadogan to Major Marsac. Twenty-five acres of garden, four hundred acres of park, six acres of kitchen garden. A large lawn, separated by a sunk fence from the garden, appears to be part of it. A straight, broad gravel walk passes before the front and parallel to it, terminated on the right by a Doric temple, and opening at the other end on a fine prospect. This straight walk has an ill effect. The lawn in front, which is pasture, well disposed with clumps of trees.

. . .

Wotton.—Now belongs to the Marquis of Buckingham, son of George Grenville. The lake covers fifty acres, the river five acres, the basin fifteen acres, the little river two acres— equal to seventy-two acres of water. The lake and great river are on a level; they fall into the basin five feet below, and that again into the little river five feet lower. These waters lie in the form of └ the house is in the middle of the open side, fronting the angle. A walk goes round the whole, three miles in circumference, and containing within it about three hun- dred acres: sometimes it passes close to the water, sometimes so far off as to leave large pasture grounds between it and the water. But two hands to keep the pleasure grounds in order; much neglected. The water affords two thousand brace of carp a year. There is a Palladian bridge, of which, I think, Whately does not speak.

. . .

Stowe.—Belongs to the Marquis of Buckingham, son of George Grenville, and who takes it from Lord Temple. Fifteen men and eighteen boys employed in keeping pleasure grounds. Within the walk are considerable portions separated by enclosures and used for pasture. The Egyptian pyramid is almost entirely taken down by the late Lord Temple, to erect a building there, in commemoration of Mr. Pitt, but he died before beginning it, and nothing is done to it yet. The grotto and two rotundas are taken away. There are four levels of water, receiving it one from the other. The basin contains seven acres, the lake below that ten acres. Kent's building is called the temple of Venus. The enclosure is entirely by ha-ha. At each end of the front line there is a recess like the bastion of a fort. In one of these is the temple of Friendship, in the other the temple of Venus. They are seen the one from the other, the line of sight passing, not through the garden, but through the country parallel to the line of the garden. This has a good effect. In the approach to Stowe, you are brought a mile through a straight avenue, pointing to the Corinthian arch and to the house, till you get to the arch, then you turn short to the right. The straight approach is very ill. The Corinthian arch has a very useless appearance, inasmuch as it has no pretension to any destination. Instead of being an object from the house, it is an obstacle to a very pleasing distant prospect. The Grecian valley being clear of trees, while the hill on each side is covered with them, is much deepened to appearance.

. . .

Leasowes, in Shropshire.—Now the property of Mr. Horne by purchase. One hundred and fifty acres within the walk. The waters small. This is not even an ornamented farm—it is only a grazing farm with a path round it, here and there a seat of board, rarely anything better. Architecture has contributed nothing. The obelisk is of brick. Shenstone had but three hundred pounds a year, and ruined himself by what he did to this farm. It is said that he died of the heart-aches which his debts occasioned him. The part next to the road is of red earth, that on the further part grey. The first and second cascades are beautiful. The landscape at number eighteen, and prospect at thirty-two, are fine. The walk through the wood is umbrageous and pleasing. The whole arch of prospect may be of ninety degrees. Many of the inscriptions are lost.

. . .

Hagley, now Lord Wescot's.—One thousand acres: no distinction between park and garden—both blended, but more of the character of garden. Eight or nine laborers keep it in order. Between two and three hundred deer in it, some of them red deer. They breed sometimes with the fallow. This garden occupying a descending hollow between the Clent and Witchbury hills, with the spurs from those hills, there is no level in it for a spacious water. There are, therefore, only some small ponds. From one of these there is a fine cascade; but it can only be, occasionally, by opening the sluice. This is in a small, dark, deep hollow, with recesses of stone in the banks on every side. In one of these is a Venus predique, turned half round as if inviting you with her into the recess. There is another cascade seen from the portico on the bridge. The castle is triangular, with a round tower at each angle, one only entire; it seems to be between forty and fifty feet high. The ponds yield a great deal of trout. The walks are scarcely gravelled.

. . .

Blenheim.—Twenty-five hundred acres, of which two hundred is garden, one hundred and fifty water, twelve kitchen garden, and the rest park. Two hundred people employed to keep it in order, and to make alterations and additions. About fifty of these employed in pleasure grounds. The turf is mowed once in ten days. In summer, about two thousand fallow deer in the park, and two or three thousand sheep. The palace of Henry II was remaining till taken down by Sarah, widow of the first Duke of Marlborough. It was on a round spot levelled by art, near what is now water, and but a little above it. The island was a part of the high road leading to the palace. Rosamond's bower was near where is now a little grove, about two hundred yards from the palace. The well is near where the bower was. The water here is very beautiful, and very grand. The cascade from the lake, a fine one; except this the garden has no great beauties. It is not laid out in fine lawns and woods, but the trees are scattered thinly over the ground, and every here and there small thickets of shrubs, in oval raised beds, cultivated, and flowers among the shrubs. The gravelled walks are broad—art appears too much. There are but a few seats in it, and nothing of architecture more dignified. There is no one striking position in it. There has been a great addition to the length of the river since Whateley wrote.

. . .

Enfield Chase.—One of the four lodges. Garden about sixty acres. Originally by Lord Chatham, now in the tenure of Dr. Beaver, who married the daughter of Mr. Sharpe. The lease lately renewed—not in good repair. The water very fine; would admit of great improvement by extending walks, etc., to the principal water at the bottom of the lawn.

. . .

Moor Park.—The lawn about thirty acres. A piece of ground up the hill of six acres. A small lake. Clumps of spruce firs. Surrounded by walk—separately inclosed [sic]—destroys unity. The property of Mr. Rous, who bought of Sir

Thomas Dundas. The building superb; the principal front a Corinthian portico of four columns; in front of the wings a colonnade, Ionic, subordinate. Back front a terrace, four Corinthian pilasters. Pulling down wings of building; removing deer; wants water.

ANDREW JACKSON DOWNING
(1815–1852)

*The first great popularizer of the American landscape,
Andrew Jackson Downing brought the concept of landscape
gardening and the importance of "taste" to everyman. He
made Americans aware of the superiority of English and
European landscape art, yet he showed how elegance and
refinement could be achieved by approaching "most nearly to
facsimiles of nature herself." Downing died tragically by
drowning in a steamboat accident at the age of thirty-seven.
This excerpt on "Treatment of Water" comes from the sixth
edition of* A Treatise on the Theory and Practice of
Landscape Gardening . . . , *1859.*

A Treatise on the Theory and Practice of Landscape Gardening

Treatment of Water

Beautiful effects of this element in nature. In what cases is it desirable to attempt the formation of artificial pieces of water. Regular forms unpleasing. Directions for the formation of ponds or lakes in the irregular manner. Study of natural lakes. Islands. Planting the margin. Treatment of natural brooks and rivulets. Cascades and waterfalls. Legitimate sphere of the art in this department.

> —*The dale*
> *With woods o'erhung, and shagg'd with mossy rocks,*
> *Whence on each hand the gushing waters play,*
> *And down the rough cascade white-dashing fall,*
> *Or gleam in lengthened vista through the trees.*
> THOMSON

The delightful and captivating effects of water in landscapes of every description are universally known and admitted. The boundless sea, the broad full river, the dashing noisy brook, and the limpid meandering rivulet, are all possessed of their peculiar charms; and when combined with scenes otherwise finely disposed and well wooded, they add a hundred fold to their beauty. The soft and trembling shadows of

Source: New York: A. O. Moore, 1859.

the surrounding trees and hills, as they fall upon a placid sheet of water—the brilliant light which the crystal surface reflects in pure sunshine, mirroring, too, at times in its resplendent bosom, all the cerulean depth and snowy whiteness of the overhanging sky, give it an almost magical effect in a beautiful landscape. The murmur of the babbling brook, that

"In linked sweetness long drawn out,"

falls upon the ear in some quiet secluded spot, is inexpressibly soothing and delightful to the mind; and the deeper sound of the cascade that rushes, with an almost musical dash, over its bed of moss-covered rock, is one of the most fascinating of the many elements of enjoyment in a fine country seat. The simplest or the most monotonous view may be enlivened by the presence of water in any considerable quantity; and the most picturesque and striking landscape will, by its addition, receive a new charm, inexpressibly enhancing all its former interest. In short, as no place can be considered perfectly complete without either a water view or water upon its own grounds, wherever it does not so exist and can be *easily* formed by artificial means, no man will neglect to take advantage of so fine a source of embellishment as is this element in some of its varied forms.

. . .

There is no department of Landscape Gardening which appears to have been less understood in this country than the management of water. Although there have not been many attempts made in this way, yet the occasional efforts that have been put forth in various parts of the country, in the shape of square, circular, and oblong pools of water, indicate a state of knowledge extremely meagre, in the art of Landscape Gardening. The highest scale to which these pieces of water rise in our estimation is that of respectable horse-ponds; beautiful objects they certainly are not. They are generally round or square, with perfectly smooth, flat banks on every side, and resemble a huge basin set down in the middle of a green lawn.

Lakes or ponds are the most beautiful forms in which water can be displayed in the grounds of a country residence.* They invariably produce their most pleasing effects when they are below the level of the house; as, if above, they are lost to the view, and if placed on a level with the eye, they are seen to much less advantage. We conceive that they should never be introduced where they do not naturally exist, except with the concurrence of the following circumstances. First, a sufficient quantity of running water to maintain *at all times* an overflow, for nothing can be more unpleasant than a stagnant pool, as nothing is more delightful than pure, clear, limpid water; and secondly, some natural formation of ground, in which the proposed water can be expanded, that will not only make it appear natural, but diminish, a hundred fold, the expense of formation.

. . .

In arranging these outlines and banks, we should study the effect at the points from which they will generally be viewed. Some pieces of water in valleys, are looked down upon from other and higher parts of the demesne; others (and this is most generally the case) are only seem from the adjoining walk, at some point or points where the latter approaches the lake. They are most generally seen from one, and seldom from more than two sides. When a lake is viewed from above, its contour should be studied as a whole; but when it is only seen from one or more sides or points, the

* Owing to the immense scale upon which nature displays this fine element in North America, every sheet of water of moderate or small size is almost universally called a *pond*. And many a beautiful, limpid, natural expanse, which in England would be thought a charming lake, is here simply a pond. The term may be equally correct, but it is by no means as elegant.

beauty of the *coup d'œil* from those positions can often be greatly increased by some trifling alterations in arrangement. A piece of water which is long and comparatively narrow, appears extremely different in opposite points of view; if seen lengthwise from either extremity, its apparent breadth and extent is much increased; while, if the spectator be placed on one side and look across, it will seem narrow and insignificant. Now, although the form of an artificial lake of moderate size should never be much less in breadth than in length, yet the contrary is sometimes unavoidably the case; and being so, we should by all means avail ourselves of those well known laws in perspective, which will place them in the best possible position, relative to the spectator.

If the improver desire to render his banks still more picturesque, resembling the choicest *morceaux* of natural banks, he should go a step further in arranging his materials before he introduces the water, or clothes the margin with vegetation. In analysing the finest portions of natural banks, it will be observed that their peculiar characteristics often depend on other objects besides the mere ground of the surrounding banks, and the trees and verdure with which they are clothed. These are, rocks of various size, forms, and colors, often projecting out of or holding up the bank in various places; stones sometimes imbedded in the soil, sometimes lying loosely along the shore; and lastly, old stumps of trees with gnarled roots, whose decaying hues are often extremely mellow and agreeable to the eye. All these have much to do with the expression of a truly picturesque bank, and cannot be excluded or taken away from it without detracting largely from its character. There is no reason, therefore, in an imitation of nature, why we should not make use of all her materials to produce a similar effect; and although in the raw and rude state of the banks at first, they may have a singular and rather *outré* aspect, stuck round and decorated here and there with large rocks, smaller stones, and old stumps of trees; yet it must be remembered that this is only the chaotic state, from which the new creation is to emerge more perfectly formed and completed; and also that the appearance of these rocks and stumps, when covered with mosses, and partially overgrown with a profusion of luxuriant vegetation and climbing plants, will be as beautifully picturesque after a little time has elapsed, as it is now uncouth and uninviting.

Islands generally contribute greatly to the beauty of a piece of water. They serve, still further, to increase the variety of outline, and to break up the wide expanse of liquid into secondary portions, without injuring the effect of the whole. The striking contrast, too, between their verdure, the color of their margins, composed of variously tinted soils and stones, and the still, smooth water around them—softened and blended as this contrast is, by their shadows reflected back from the limpid element, gives additional richness to the picture.

The distribution of islands in a lake or pond requires some judgment. They will always appear more natural when sufficiently near the shore, on either side, to maintain in appearance some connexion [sic] with it. Although islands do sometimes occur near the middle of natural lakes, yet the effect is by no means good, as it not only breaks and distracts the effects of the whole expanse by dividing it into two distinct parts, but it always indicates a shallowness or want of depth where the water should be deepest.

There are two situations where it is universally admitted that islands may be happily introduced. These are, at the inlet and the exit of the body of water. In many cases where the stream which supplies the lake is not remarkable for size, and will add nothing to the appearance of the whole view from the usual points of sight, it may be concealed by an island or small group of islands, placed at some little distance

14

in front of it. The head or dam of a lake, too, is often necessarily so formal and abrupt, that it is difficult to make it
appear natural and in good keeping with the rest of the
margin. The introduction of an island or two, placed near
the main shore, on either side, and projecting as far as possible before the dam, will greatly diminish this disagreeable
formality, particularly if well clothed with a rich tuft of shrubs
and overhanging bushes.

Except in these two instances, islands should be generally placed *opposite the salient points* of the banks, or near those
places where small breaks or promontories run out into the
water. In such situations, they will increase the regularity of
the outline, and lend it additional spirit and animation.
Should they, on the other hand, be seated in or near the
marginal curve and indentations, they will only serve to clog
up these recesses; and while their own figures are lost in
these little bays where they are hidden, by lessening the already existing irregularities, they will render the whole outline tame and spiritless.

On one or two of these small islands, little rustic habitations, if it coincide with the taste of the proprietor, may be
made for different aquatic birds or waterfowl, which will
much enliven the scene by their fine plumage. Among these
the *swan* is pre-eminent, for its beauty and gracefulness.
Abroad, they are the almost constant accompaniments of water in the ground of country residences; and it cannot be
denied that, floating about in the limpid wave, with their
snow-white plumage and superbly curved necks, they are
extremely elegant objects.

After having arranged the banks, reared up the islands,
and completely formed the bed of the proposed lake, the
improver will next proceed, at the proper period, to finish
his labors by clothing the newly formed ground, in various
parts, with vegetation. This may be done immediately, if it be

desirable; or if the season be not favorable, it may be deferred until the banks, and all the newly formed earth, have had time to settle and assume their final forms, after the dam has been closed, and the whole basin filled to its intended height.

Planting the margins of pieces of water, if they should be of much extent, must evidently proceed upon the same leading principle that we have already laid down for ornamental plantations in other situations. That is, there must be trees of different heights and sizes, and underwood and shrubs of lower growth, disposed sometimes singly, at others in masses, groups, and thickets: in all of which forms, *connexion* [sic] must be preserved, and the whole must be made to blend well together, while the different sizes and contours will prevent any sameness and confusion. On the retreating dry banks, the taller and more sturdy deciduous and evergreen trees, as the oak, ash, etc., may be planted, and nearer by, the different willows, the elm, the alder, and other trees that love a moister situation, will thrive well. It is indispensably necessary, in order to produce breadth of effect and strong rich contrasts, that *underwood* should be employed to clothe many parts of the banks. Without it, the stems of trees will appear loose and straggling, and the screen will be so imperfect as to allow a free passage for the vision in every direction. For this purpose, we have in all our woods, swamps, and along our brooks, an abundance of hazels, hawthorns, alders, spice woods, winter berries, azaleas, spireas, and a hundred other fine low shrubs, growing wild, which are by nature extremely well fitted for such sites, and will produce immediate effect on being transplanted. These may be intermingled, here and there, with the swamp button-bush (*Cephalanthus*), which bears handsome white globular heads of blossoms, and the swamp magnolia, which is highly beautiful and fragrant. On cool north banks, among shelves of proper soil upheld by projecting ledges of rock, our native Kalmias and Rhododendrons, the common and mountain laurels, may be made to flourish. The Virginia Creeper, and other beautiful wild vines, may be planted at the roots of some of the trees to clamber up their stems, and the wild Clematis so placed that its luxuriant festoons shall hang gracefully from the projecting boughs of some of the overarching trees. Along the lower banks and closer margins, the growth of smaller plants will be encouraged, and various kinds of wild ferns may be so planted as partially to conceal, overrun, and hide the rocks and stumps of trees while trailing plants, as the periwinkle and moneywort (*Lysamachia nummularia*) [sic], will still further increase the intricacy and richness of such portions. In this way, the borders of the lake will resemble the finest portions of the banks of picturesque and beautiful natural dells and pieces of water, and the effect of the whole when time has given it the benefit of its softening touches, if it has been thus properly executed, will not be much inferior to those matchless bits of fine landscape. A more striking and artistical effect will be produced by substituting for native trees and shrubs, common on the banks of streams and lakes in the country, only rare *foreign* shrubs, vines, and aquatic plants of hardy growth, suitable for such situations. While these are arranged in the same manner as the former, from their comparative novelty, especially in such sites, they will at once convey the idea of refined and elegant art.

If any person will take the trouble to compare a piece of water so formed, when complete, with the square or circular sheets or ponds now in vogue among us, he must indeed be little gifted with an appreciation of the beautiful, if he do not at once perceive the surpassing merit of the natural style. In the old method, the banks, level, or rising on all sides, without any but few surrounding trees, carefully gravelled along the edge of the water, or what is still worse, walled up, slope away in a tame, dull, uninteresting grass field. In the natural method, the outline is varied, sometimes receding from the eye, at others stealing out, and inviting the gaze—the banks here slope off gently with a gravelly beach, and there rise abruptly in different heights, abounding with hollows, projections, and eminences, showing various colored rocks and soils, intermingled with a luxuriant vegetation of all sizes and forms, corresponding to the different situations. Instead of allowing the sun to pour down in one blaze of light, without any objects to soften it with their shade, the thick overhanging groups and masses of trees cast, here and there, deep cool shadows. Stealing through the leaves and branches, the sun-beams quiver and play upon the surface of the flood, and are reflected back in dancing light, while their full glow upon the broader and more open portions of the lake is relieved, and brought into harmony by the cooler and softer tints mirrored in the water from the surrounding hues and tints of banks, rocks, and vegetation.

. . .

From all that we have suggested in these limited remarks, it will be seen that we would only attempt in our operations with water, the graceful or picturesque imitations of natural lakes or ponds, and brooks, rivulets, and streams. Such are the only forms in which this unrivalled element can be displayed so as to harmonize agreeably with natural and picturesque scenery. In the latter, there can be no apology made for the introduction of straight canals, round or oblong pieces of water, and all the regular forms of the geometric mode; because they would evidently be in violent opposition to the whole character and expression of natural landscape. In architectural, or flower gardens (on which we shall hereafter have occasion to offer some remarks), where a different and highly artificial arrangement prevails, all these regular forms, with various jets, foundations, etc., may be employed with good taste, and will combine well with the other accessories of such places. But in the grounds of a residence in the modern style, *nature,* if possible, still more purified, as in the great *chefs-d'œuvre* of art, by an ideal standard, should be the great aim of the Landscape Gardener. And with water especially, only beautiful when allowed to take its own flowing forms and graceful motions, more than with any other of our materials, all appearance of constraint and formality should be avoided. If art be at all manifest, it should discover itself only, as in the admirably painted landscape, in the reproduction of nature in her choicest developments. Indeed, many of the most celebrated authors who have treated of this subject, appear to agree that the productions of the artist in this branch are most perfect as they approach most nearly to facsimiles of nature herself: and though art should have formed the whole, its employment must be nowhere discovered by the spectator; or as *Tasso* has more elegantly expressed the idea:

"L'arte che tutto fa, nulla si scopre."

FREDERICK LAW OLMSTED
(1822–1903)

Frederick Law Olmsted is the best-known American landscape architect, a term that he coined in order to dignify a relatively new profession. He is justly famous for his design, with Calvert Vaux, of New York's Central Park, which set a standard for urban park design throughout the country. The inspiration for this masterpiece came on a trip to England, where he visited "The People's Park" at Birkenhead, near Liverpool, in May 1851.

WALKS AND TALKS OF AN AMERICAN FARMER IN ENGLAND

The baker had begged of us not to leave Birkenhead without seeing their New Park, and at his suggestion we left our knap-sacks with him, and proceeded to it. As we approached the entrance, we were met by women and girls, who, holding out a cup of milk, asked us—"Will you take a cup of milk, sirs? Good, cool, sweet cow's milk, gentlemen, or right warm from the ass!" And at the gate was a herd of donkeys, some with cans of milk strapped to them, others saddled and bridled, to be let for ladies and children to ride.

The gateway, which is about a mile and a half from the ferry and quite back of the town, is a great, massive block of handsome Ionic architecture, standing alone, and unsupported by any thing else in the vicinity, and looking, as I think, heavy and awkward. There is a sort of grandeur about it that the English are fond of, but which, when it is entirely separate from all other architectural constructions, always strikes me unpleasantly. It seems intended as an impressive preface to a great display of art within; but here, as well as at Easton Park, and other places I have since seen, it is not followed up with great things, the grounds immediately within the grand entrance being simple and apparently rather overlooked by the gardener. There is a large archway for carriages, and two smaller ones for people on foot, and, on either side, and over these, are rooms which probably serve as inconvenient lodges for the laborers. No porter appears, and the gates are freely opened to the public.

Walking a short distance up an avenue, we passed

Source: New York: Rikei, Thorne and Company, 1854.

through another light iron gate into a thick, luxuriant, and diversified garden. Five minutes of admiration, and a few more spent in studying the manner in which art had been employed to obtain from nature so much beauty, and I was ready to admit that in democratic America there was nothing to be thought of as comparable with this People's Garden. Indeed, gardening had here reached a perfection that I had never before dreamed of. I cannot undertake to describe the effect of so much taste and skill as had evidently been employed; I will only tell you, that we passed by winding paths, over acres and acres, with a constant varying surface, where on all sides were growing every variety of shrubs and flowers, with more than natural grace, all set in borders of greenest, closest turf, and all kept with most consummate neatness. At a distance of a quarter of a mile from the gate, we came to an open field of clean, bright, green-sward, closely mown, on which a large tent was pitched, and a party of boys in on one part, and a party of gentlemen in another, were playing cricket. Beyond this was a large meadow with groups of young trees, under which a flock of sheep were reposing, and girls and women with children, were playing. While watching the cricketers, we were threatened with a shower, and hastened to look for shelter, which we found in a pagoda, on an island approached by a Chinese bridge. It was soon filled, as were the other ornamental buildings, by a crowd of those who, like ourselves, had been overtaken in the grounds by the rain; and I was glad to observe that the privileges of the garden were enjoyed about equally by all classes. There were some who were attended by servants, and sent at once for their carriages, but a large proportion were of the common ranks, and a few woman with children, or suffering from ill health, were evidently the wives of very humble laborers. There were a number of strangers and some we observed with note-books and portfolios, who seemed to have come from a distance to study in the garden. The summer-houses, lodges, bridges, etc., were all well constructed, and of unde-caying materials. One of the bridges which we crossed was of our countryman Remington's patent, an extremely light and graceful erection.

I obtained most of the following information from the head working-gardener.

The site of the park and garden was, ten years ago, a flat, clay farm. It was placed in the hands of Mr. Paxton, in June, 1844, by whom it was roughly laid out in its present form by June of the following year.* Carriage roads, 34 feet wide, with borders of ten feet, and walks varying in width, were first drawn and made. The excavation for a pond was also immediately undertaken, and the earth ob-tained from these sources used for making mounds and to vary the surface, which has been done with much natural-ness. The whole ground was thoroughly under-drained, the minor drains of stone, the main of tile. By these sufficient water is obtained to fully supply the pond, or lake, as they call it, which is from twenty to forty feet wide and about three feet deep, and meanders for a long distance through the garden. It is stocked with aquatic plants, goldfish, and swans.

The roads are macadamized. On each side of the car-riage way, and of all the walks, pipes for drainage are laid, which communicate with deep main drains that run under the edge of all the mounds or flower beds. The walks are laid first with six inches of fine broken stone, then three inches cinders, and the surface with six inches of fine rolled gravel. All the stones on the ground which were not used for these purposes, were laid in masses of rock-work, and mosses and rock-plants attached to them. The mounds were finally

---

* Mr. Kemp has the credit of the design with the public. I suppose that he was employed by Paxton to perfect his plan and superintend the construction.

planted with shrubs, and heaths and ferns, and the beds with
flowering plants. Between these and the walks and drives, is
everywhere a belt of turf (which, by the way, is kept close cut
with short, broad scythes, and shears, and swept with *hair-
brooms,* as we saw). Then the rural lodges, temples, pavillion,
bridges, orchestra for a band of instrumental music, etc.,
were built. And so, in one year, the skeleton of this delightful
garden was complete.

But this is but a small part. Besides the cricket and an
archery ground, large valleys were made verdant, extensive
drives arranged—plantations, clumps, and avenues of trees
formed, and a large park laid out. And all this magnificent
pleasure ground is entirely, unreservedly, and for ever, the
people's own. The poorest British peasant is as free to enjoy
it in all its parts as the British queen. More than that, the
baker of Birkenhead has the pride of an owner in it.

Is it not a grand, good thing? But you are inquiring who
paid for it. The honest owners—the most wise and worthy
townspeople of Birkenhead—in the same way that the New
Yorkers pay for "the Tombs," and the Hospital, and the
cleaning (as they say) of their streets.

Of the farm which was purchased, one hundred twenty
acres have been disposed of in the way I have described.
The remaining sixty acres, encircling the park and garden,
were reserved to be sold or rented, after being well graded,
streeted, and planted, for private building lots. Several fine
mansions are already built on these (having private entrances to the park), and the rest now sell at $1.25 a square
yard. The whole concern cost the town between five and six
hundred thousand dollars. It gives employment at present
to ten gardeners and laborers in summer, and to five in
winter.

The generous spirit and fearless enterprise that has ac-
complished this, has not been otherwise forgetful of the

health and comfort of the poor.* Among other things, I remember, a public washing and bathing house for the town is provided. I should have mentioned also, in connection with the market, that in the outskirts of the town there is a range of stone slaughter-houses with stables, yards, pens, supplies of hot and cold water, and other arrangements and conveniences, that enlightened regard for health and decency would suggest.

The consequence of all these sorts of things is that all about the town, lands, which a few years ago were almost worthless wastes, have become of priceless value; where no sound was heard but the bleating of goats and braying of asses complaining of their pasturage, there is now the hasty click and clatter of many hundred busy trowels and hammers. You may drive through wide and thronged streets of stately edifices, where were only a few scattered huts, surrounded by quagmires. Docks of unequaled size and grandeur are building, and a forest of masts grow along the shore; and there is no doubt that this young town is to be not only remarkable as a most agreeable and healthy place of residence, but that it will soon be distinguished for extensive and profitable commerce. It seems to me to be the only town I ever saw that has been really built at all in accordance with the advanced science, taste, and enterprising spirit that are supposed to distinguish the nineteenth century. I do not doubt it might be found to have plenty of exceptions to its general character, but I did not inquire for these, nor did I happen to observe them. Certainly, in what I have noticed, it is a model town, and may be held up as an example, not only to philanthropists and men of taste, but to speculators and men of business.

* "Few towns, in modern times, have been built with such regard to sanitary regulations as Birkenhead; and in no instance has so much been done for the health, comfort, and enjoyment of a people as by these energetic individuals with whose names the rise and progress of Birkenhead are so intimately connected."—Dr. J.H. Robertson.

After leaving the park, we ascended a hill, from the top of which we had a fine view of Liverpool and Birkenhead. Its sides were covered with villas, with little gardens about them. The architecture was generally less fantastic, and the style and materials of building more substantial, than is usually employed in the same class of residences with us. Yet there was a good deal of the same *stuck-up* and uneasy pretentious air about them that the suburban houses of our own city people so commonly have. Possibly this is the effect of association, in my mind, of steady, reliable worth and friendship with plain or old-fashioned dwellings, for I often find it difficult to discover in the buildings themselves the elements of such expression. I am inclined to think it is more generally owing to some disunity in the design—often, perhaps, to a want of keeping between the mansion and its grounds, or its situation. The architect and the gardener do not understand each other, and commonly the owner or resident is totally at variance in his tastes and intentions from both; or the man whose ideas the plan is made to serve, or who pays for it, has no true, independent taste, but had fancies to be accommodated, which only follow confusedly after custom or fashion. I think, with Ruskin, it is a pity that every man's house cannot be really his own, and that he cannot make all that is true, beautiful, and good in his own character, tastes, pursuits, and history, manifest in it.

But however fanciful and uncomfortable many of the villa houses about Liverpool and Birkenhead appear at first sight, the substantial and thorough manner in which most of them are built will atone for many faults. The friendship of nature has been secured for such. Dampness, heat, cold, will be welcome to do their best; every day they will improve. In fifty or a hundred years fashion may change, and they will appear, perhaps, quaint, possibly grotesque; but still strong, home-like, and hospitable. They have no shingles to rot, no glued and puttied and painted gimcrackery, to warp and crack and molder; and can never look so shabby, and desolate, and dreary, as will nine-tenths of the buildings of the same denomination now erecting about New York, almost as soon as they lose the raw, cheerless, impostorlike airs which seem inseparable from their newness.

THOMAS MEEHAN
(1826–1901)

Described as one of the most brilliant horticulturists of his time, Meehan worked on the renovation of John Bartram's garden and prepared a list of trees growing there. He expanded this information into The American Handbook of Ornamental Trees *(1853). The American ideal for comfort in living is the single-family residence, set in a gracious greensward, surrounded by beautiful shade trees. Perhaps Meehan started all of this. He certainly gave the idea a great deal of encouragement.*

THE AMERICAN HANDBOOK
OF ORNAMENTAL TREES

Trees are essential to an American home. The frame
building, the first pointer to the young mechanic in his ar-
duous path towards an honorable independence, is imperfect without the idea of shade trees surrounding it. And
when, as he proceeds onwards, prosperity and plenty, smiling on his genius and on his talents, suggest the idea of a
suburban residence, he dwells with pleasure on the vast
variety of ornamental flowering trees, producing each
month a succession of beautiful novelties, clothed with an
endless variety of ever-changing foliage, administering
equally shade and shelter for the body with food and enjoyment for the mind, which are pictured with it. Perhaps
fortune has chosen him one of her special favorites. He becomes a man of wealth. Being a man of taste, endowed with
an active sympathy for the charms of nature; alive to the
keenest relish for landscape beauties; he has seen in his
travels some of the fairest specimens of nature's handiwork
in forest scenery, and resolved on forming a country-seat
where he

>"—with unsparing hand,
> May cull the beauties of each land,
> And blend them in that favored spot,"

and aim at producing in one whole a pleasing picture of
garden scenery, out of the materials nature has scattered so
bountifully in various parts of the world.

. . .

Source: Philadelphia: Lippincott, Grambo, and Co., 1853.

On the Selection of All Kinds of Trees

Firstly, we have to consider what the tree is wanted for; whether for shade, for ornament, or both combined; for utility or beauty; whether a rapid growth be desired, or the highest effects of the art without reference to time; whether they are to be planted singly, or together in masses?

A shade tree should have a widely spreading head, abundant leaves, or dense foliage. It should bud forth early in spring and retain its leaves late in autumn. It should also be free from unpleasant odors, and liability to attacks of disease or insects. All fruit-trees are objectionable. Who would choose a Lombardy poplar for a shade tree? The honey-locust has too fine a foliage. The odor of the ailanthus is unpleasant. The Kentucky coffee buds late, and the American buttonwood is too unhealthy. Still, there is great scope for variety. Fine selections can be made from amongst the horse-chestnuts and buckeyes, maples, some birches, ashes, tulip-tree, magnolias, hop horn-bean, English buttonwood, the oaks, sweet-chestnut, sophora, and in some parts or situations, lindens and willows.

But it is by no means in the majority of cases that trees are planted for the mere luxury of the shade they afford, or their utility in screening disagreeable objects. They are valued for the effect they have on the landscape; the beauty they exhibit in their forms; the cheerfulness that dwells in their foliage; the gayety that bursts from their opening blossoms, charms; and the contrasts they make with each other, please. To these, if they combine harmony with surrounding objects, expression of the artist's ideas, or association with classic history, or remarkable occurrences, they afford additional interest. These are points which few can master thoroughly, without long and careful study. Yet, on the perfection of this knowledge, depends the production of the most pleasing effects from ornamental arboriculture.

The effect to be produced by trees, should be particularly well studied. The object must never be lost sight of. Pleasure, in its broadest sense, is generally a main object; this is always to be derived from a perception of the beautiful. Unity, harmony, and appropriate fitness, are the essential elements of beauty; to these, then, must the planter's efforts turn.

The relation or fitness of a tree to the subject in connection with it, will be one of first importance in the study of effect. A tree, beautiful in some situations, and in connection with some objects, will fail to please under other circumstances. A tree out of character is as offensive to the cultivated mind as would be a dress of the finest satin on the back of a beggar. So, an idea attached to a tree by association, gives it a character which cannot be removed from it without violence. A traveller, accustomed to associate the cypress or yew-tree with churchyards or monuments, would be painfully struck on meeting an avenue of them leading to a mansion. The same ideas hold good in the peculiar character of trees, as well as in their associations. A magnificent deodar, or even a Norway spruce, solitary and alone, would look as ridiculous by the side of one of our western log-houses as a noble, weather-beaten, rustic-looking oak would alongside a magnificent modern specimen of city architecture.

We often hear the remark that evergreens around a mansion look so beautiful. Others again give a decided preference to deciduous trees. This difference of opinion can be accounted for on philosophical principles, and does not originate from any variation in the principles of beauty. Evergreens are the accompaniments of the thoughtful and the reflective. As we advance in age, the fondness for them grows more devoted. Their unchanging character suits the reflective steadiness that characterizes old age, and which draws our affection towards them as to bosom friends. Deciduous trees are emblematic of lightness and gayety; the young and untutored will always prefer them. Our happiest remembrances cling around the old oak of our childhood's home, without a thought or a care for the holly or the pine.

For these reasons evergreens should never preponderate around places, or in situations devoted to amusement or recreation. By schools, or places devoted to the young, they are objectionable in great numbers. Unsuggestive of lightness and gayety, they are opposed to the thoughtless, yet happy innocence of childhood. Wherever the aged love to resort, whatever is to have an air of solitude or peace, there is the spot which evergreens will adorn; here is the point from which they will really seem beautiful.

The selection of trees for effect can then depend upon no particular rule, fitness or appropriateness depending upon each circumstance; but unity and harmony are more general in their application.

Unity of design must not degenerate into formality; nor harmony into monotony. It is the frequency of this degeneracy that produces the opposite errors of irregularity and discord. One, in a mistaken view of unity, will divide his grounds into two equal parts, and an oak or an elm on one side must have precisely the same on the other, as if to balance the whole. Another, disgusted with such abortions of taste, plunges into the opposite error. His place has the appearance of having fallen into the hands of men of all principles, ages, and nations, each one of whom had successively stuck on a patch, till, between the daubs of so many brushes on their objectional part of the picture, little of the original design is left.

Variety is not opposed to unity. The oneness should be

in the outline; the more varied, then, the filling up, the better. The carriage entrance to an old mansion is often improved by a row of trees on each side. Each set of two placed opposite to one another should of course correspond. One would as soon see beauty in one gate-post, or one eye being larger than the other, as to see anything different in this respect. Yet there could be no objection to the successive sets of trees varying in species or varieties, so long as no rule of harmony was broken thereby. A light, airy-looking tree, like the hemlock-spruce, should not be placed immediately after a rugged, artificial-looking Norway. Its gracefulness would be in part absorbed by the rusticity of the latter, and both lose by comparison.

This harmony of color, shade, and contrast, is of more importance in the general arrangement of trees in a garden than in such an avenue as I have described. They are to be looked at in greater masses, seen from more distant points of view, or from more varied positions.

The colors, tints, and hues of the foliage at different seasons of the year, will then have to be more particularly studied. Much may be lost or gained in the effect of a single tree. The golden hue of a sugar maple in the fall, appears to great advantage followed by a sassafras with its rosy yellow tints; and this, again, followed by a red or swamp maple or tupelo, forms a beautiful combination. If we were to take away the sassafras and replace it with a British oak, the effect would be anything but pleasing.

Not only in color should there be harmony, but also in height, habit, and appearance. All violent contrasts are opposed to natural beauty. In the oft-quoted language of Ray,* "nature never takes leaps," but proceeds gradually step by step. Differing in variety, yet united in general principles,

* Ray, Rev. John (1627–1705). English clergyman and author of *British Flora.*—Ed.

each clump or section of trees in a landscape will possess characteristics exclusively its own. Few mistakes can arise from planting trees simply; harmony and association with the objects alone being called for.

In planting for a wood or grove, it is frequently the desire to make a small place look larger. Every bend should possess some new or striking feature. A long walk around a wood will not please without an object. A visitor may be surprised at the extent, but to the proprietor it is wearisome. His pleasure can only be secured by a succession of ever present, yet ever changing objects of beauty along the course.

Thus the plant should be imbued with the principles of beauty. Without them his labors may excite only wonder at their extent, or surprise at their variety; with them, he combines lasting beauty—a source of unvarying pleasure and delight.

CHARLES HOWARD SHINN
(1852–1924)

The Pacific Rural Handbook *was published in San
Francisco in 1879, scarcely a quarter century after
California became a state. This was the first garden book for
these "new dwellers in Arcadia." Charles Shinn cautions
against all the excesses of planting, which now characterize
so much of the California suburban landscape. "Neither
should any man expect to buy all the different species which
are for sale at the nurseries, any more than he desires to
wear all the new styles of cravat on one occasion."
Good advice, poorly received!*

PACIFIC RURAL HANDBOOK

*Containing a Series of Brief and Practical Essays
and Notes on the Culture of Trees, Vegetables and
Flowers, Adapted to the Pacific Coast. Also Hints
on Home and Farm Improvements.*

Laying Out the Grounds

Innate Love of Rural Life.—The Pleasantness of
Founding a Home.—We can Read Men's Character
in their Homes.—Value of Originality.—Importance of a well Considered Plan.—Hints on General
Effects and Results.

Whoever, in this fair State of ours, has become the fortunate owner of a little nook of land which, by patient and well
directed toil, may be changed from a waste to a garden, must
feel in some degree as if he were the master of a new and
glorious world. There lie the fresh and smoking furrows,
smiling to think of the countless secrets they hide—the fruit
and leaves and flowers, the shaded walks and the sloping
lawns; there the new master plans in faith and patience for
the golden years of a long and useful life. The founding of a
home is one of the purest joys left to fallen man; it is the
blessing which came softly out of Paradise with Adam, and
has followed his wandering children ever since.

. . .

Men have a curious habit of stamping their personality
on the clothes they wear, the team they drive, the house

Source: San Francisco: Dewey & Co., Publishers of the Pacific Rural Press, 1879.

they live in, and all their property, real or personal. In a most complete sense the grounds a man lays out, takes care of, and enjoys, become like himself, or rather, in a very precise way, give us glimpses of his nature, and hints of his possibilities. Indeed I love to notice the constant changes and little improvements in every village through which I pass, and make wondering guesses concerning the owners of each successive cottage. Altheas, lilacs, a damask rose, groups of pansies, and clambering wealth of sweet peas, with perhaps a sugar maple, evidently cherished—it is in some way a suggestion of a New England family. An Irish yew tree by the gate, a row of black currants along the fence, Shropshire damsons and Kentish cherries in the orchard, box borders, and Covent Garden stocks,—this is staid, portly old England, surely. Bottle gourds over the well, balsams and crape myrtle by the door, melons and gumbo in the vegetable garden—here is a picture from the sunny South. Dill, saffron, yellow marigolds, sunflowers, and horse-beans, in straight rows in front of a door painted red, yellow and blue—this can only be a Portuguese family from the Azores. It is the charm of California in the eyes of her children that so many variations are possible here, so many widely different types of gardening succeed, and blend harmoniously in our landscapes.

Secondly, therefore, I would impress originality, alike upon the young householder planning his first home, and on the busy farmer, who has probably sold out, and bought again, a dozen times during his life. The best and happiest plan to be found elsewhere ought to have some modification to suit the place, or the owner. Indeed there is little hope for you without a lively discontent with other men's plans. If you have in your nature the capacity of founding a beautiful home, you shall search volumes of landscape gardening, and find nothing fit to accept without change. A few great principles must always guide you, and suggestions from number-less sources must unite in your mind before you realize the difficulties of the work and the happiness of a successful result. You will not ever be able to say that your work is well done in the sense in which an artist speaks of a picture as finished when it leaves the easel, for you will always be haunted by growing and boundless possibilities; but when your ideas are broadly planned, and fulfilled to the earliest fruit and shade, we may safely speak of results.

The most important question to be settled at first, is, how much of the land surrounding the house is to be devoted to ornamentals, how much to fruit, and how much to out-buildings? Or, to put this in another form, what proportion shall the shrubs, flowers, and trees, bear to the whole space available? The answer to this question will depend somewhat on the state of a man's purse, but more on his feelings in the matter, since, by choosing fruit and nut-bearing trees, the poorest man may afford to surround his house with shade and beauty. Some styles of architecture, as the Italian villa, seem to require more foliage around them than others, so that this proportion ought really to be settled with some reference to the plan of the house.

More than a few good people have a theory that it is only necessary to begin work, and a successful plan will evolve itself—the buildings, paths, and beds, will assume the best positions by a series of fortunate accidents; thus, it is also believed, an air of simplicity and naturalness will be secured. But this plausible theory is a delusion. No place will ever be satisfactory if the plan is allowed to drift helplessly according to circumstances; for paths will take undirected curves, scattered beds will fail to have unity of effect, choice trees will be crowded in, without any view to the future, continual change will be needed, and a wreck on the rocks of confusion will probably end the unguided endeavor. It is best, therefore, to fully understand what you propose to do. The general plan must be well considered, and, on all important matters, settled, before a tree is planted. Haste here will prove to have been sowing a large crop of future repentance. Of course minor changes are admissible, but a definite, vital, and organized plan will need few alterations.

The next step is to find out all you can about your soil and climate, and, taking the best works obtainable, to make lists of suitable trees, shrubs, and plants. Make it much longer than you expect to use at first. Go and see fine plants at the leading nurseries, and on private grounds. If you want anything which you cannot procure from your own nurserymen, tell them so, and they will probably procure it the next season. Try to realize how each tree you think of using will look when it is fully grown. Beautiful grounds are only to be obtained by knowing beforehand nearly what effect will be produced, so that, whilst others are surprised, the quiet owner is only justified in his own thoughts by the fulfilled, but long foreshadowed, landscape.

This art of graceful combinations is the hardest, yet loveliest, of garden problems. The trees and plants of any country harmonize perfectly with each other when in their native woods, but our eagerness for new things, and our thirst for variety, often leads us to mingle the plants of every region on one poor half acre. The possibilities of artistic landscape-gardening which our climate affords, are wonderful, but the dangers also are great. Our native lilies, shrubs, and spicy vines, are perfectly at home near a drooping redwood, or mountain pine, but they have little sympathy with a Eucalyptus, other than the mere vegetable kinship. Plants, in themselves beautiful, may be, and often are, a positive injury to a garden, because they introduce an inharmonious idea in outline, style, or color. No man should ever buy a plant merely because of a vague impression that it is cheap, or pretty, or can be utilized somewhere; but he ought to know beforehand exactly where to put it, and exactly what he expects it to do in the way of harmonious effect. Neither should any man expect to buy all the different species which are for sale at the nurseries, any more than he desires to wear all the new styles of cravat on one occasion.

It is always desirable to grade the ground before any trees are planted, so that there are no little depressions where water will stand after a long rain. Do not try to produce a dead level, but uniform slopes, preserving the salient features of the location. This grading process is essential if much irrigation is proposed. By studying the surface carefully after a heavy rain the work can be done reasonably well without expensive surveying.

In arranging for the general plan it is best to avoid a carriage-road passing in a circle around the house, for the privilege of possessing your back-door in privacy is not one to be lightly cast away. Those straight roads which pass from the main gate, and go inflexibly to the stable, are only allowable on the plea of saving ground. Straight walks and rows of trees increase the sense of length, whilst curving walks and masses of shrubbery tend to diminish it. Tall trees appear best near the middle of grounds, or forming a background for buildings. Trees with feathery, graceful leaves ought to stand where their outlines are revealed against the sky. Dark and massive trees give form and stability to the landscape. The weeping trees add the sad minor key. Columnar trees should rise from masses of enveloping shrubbery. Trees with red winter-berries, as the mountain ash, and holly, show well among deciduous trees. Each tree should have room to develop its true character, and must not be tortured, by too much pruning, into a stiff and ungainly satire upon itself. Numerous hints of this kind may be given, but we can sum them all up in two precepts: "So plan your grounds that they will form one harmonious whole." "Give your grounds a positive character, suitable in general to the age we live in, and the climate we enjoy, and, in particular, to the house you have built, and your own individual tastes."

CELIA THAXTER
(1835–1894)

First published in 1894, with pictures and illuminations by Childe Hassam, An Island Garden *is an inspiration to the art and craft of garden making. In this excerpt, Celia Thaxter revels in the beauty of the annual poppies, not only admiring them in all their multifarious color, but explaining how to grow them and distinguishing between the varieties for various landscape uses. Although her garden, on Appledore Island, has been recently restored, the spirit of her gardening is expressed most vividly and beautifully in the charming paintings of Childe Hassam.*

AN ISLAND GARDEN

Much thought should be given to the garden's arrangement with regard to the economy of room where one has but a small space to devote to it. And where one is unfamiliar with the habits of growth of the various plants that are to people it, a difficulty arises in making them effective and so disposing them that they shall not interfere with each other. For instance, in most cases tall plants should be put back against walls and fences and so forth, with the lower-growing varieties in the foreground. If one were to plant Verbenas and Venidium among Sunflowers and Hollyhocks, or even among Carnation Poppies and Cornflowers, Verbenas and Venidium would not be visible for their habit is to creep close to the ground, and the tall growths would completely hide and most likely exterminate them by shutting from them the sun and air without which they cannot live. These low, creeping plants are, however, very useful when one is planning for a succession of flowers. I plant Pansies, Verbenas, Drummond's Phlox, and so forth, among my Pinks and Wallflowers and others of like compact habit, so that, when the higher slender plants have done blossoming, the others, which seldom cease flowering till frost, may still clothe the ground with color and beauty. Of course, it goes without saying that climbing Vines should not be set where there is nothing upon which they may climb. Indeed that would be simple cruelty—nothing more nor less. Everything that needs it should be given a support without fail—all the myriad lovely Vines that one may have with so little trouble, and which seem to have been made to wreathe the dwellings of men with freshness

Source: Boston: Houghton Mifflin Company, 1894.

and beauty and grace. The long list of varieties of flowering Clematis, so many shapes and colors, the numerous Honeysuckles, the Wistaria, Passion-flowers, Morning-glories, Hops, the Dutchman's Pipe, the Cobœas, Woodbine, and many others, not counting Sweet Peas and Nasturtiums— these last among the most beautiful and decorative of all,— every one is twice as valuable if given the support it demands. In the case of Nasturtiums, however, which seem with endless good-nature ready to adapt themselves to any conditions of existence, except, perhaps, being expected to live in a swamp, it is not so important that they should have something upon which to climb. A very good way is to put them near a rock one wishes to have covered, or to let them run down a bank upon which nothing else cares to grow. They will clothe such places with wild and beautiful luxuriance of green leaves and glowing flowers.

It seems strange to write a book about a little garden only fifty feet long and by fifteen wide! But then, as a friend pleasantly remarked to me, "it extends upward," and what it lacks in area is more than compensated by the large joy that grows out of it and its uplifting and refreshment of "the Spirit of Man."

. . .

I have not room to experiment with rockworks and ribbon-borders and the like, nor should I do it even if I had all the room in the world. For mine is just a little old-fashioned garden where the flowers come together to praise the Lord and to teach all who look upon them to do likewise.

All through the months of April and May, when the weather is not simply impossible, I am at work in it, and also through most of June. It is wonderful how much work one can find to do in so tiny a plot of ground. But in the latter weeks of June there comes a time when I can begin to take breath and rest a little from these difficult yet pleasant labors; an interval when I may take time to consider, a morning when I may seek the hammock in the shady piazza, and, looking across my happy flower beds, let the sweet day sink deep into my heart. From the flower beds I look over the island slopes to the sea, and realize it all,—the rapture of growth, the delicious shades of green that clothe the ground, Wild Rose, Bayberry, Spirea, Shadbush, Elder, and many more. How beautiful they are, these grassy, rocky slopes shelving gradually to the sea, with here and there a mass of tall, blossoming grass softly swaying in the warm wind against the peaceful, pale blue water! Among the grass a few ghostly dandelion tops yet linger, with now and then a belated golden flower. How lovely is the delicacy of the white bleached rocks, the little spaces of shallow soil exquisite with vivid crimson Sorrel, or pearly with the brave Eyebright, all against the soft color of the sea. What harmony of movement in all these radiant growths just stirred by the gentle air! Here and there a stout little bough of Chokecherry, with clustered white blossoms tipped with pink, springing from a cleft in the rock, lights up in sunshine, its pink more glowing for the turquoise background of the ocean. How hot the sun blazes! The Blue-eyed Grass is quite faint and drooping in the rich turf, but the yellow Crowfoot shines strong and steady; no sunshine is too bright for it. In the garden the tall Jacqueminot Rose-bushes gather power from the great warmth and light, and hold out their thick buds to absorb it and fold its splendor in their inmost hearts. One or two of the heaviest buds begin to loosen their crimson velvet petals and shed their delicious perfume on the air. The Oriental Poppy glories in the heat. Among its buds, thrust upward like solid green apples, one has burst into burning flame, each of its broad fiery petals as large as the whole inside of my hand. In the Iceland Poppy bed the ardent light has wooed a graceful company of drooping buds to blow, and their cups of delicate fire, orange and yellow, sway lightly on stems as slender as grass. In sheltered corners the Forget-me-not spreads its cool, heaven-blue clusters; by the fence "the Larkspurs listen" while they wait; the large purple Pansies shrink and turn from the too brilliant gaze of the sun. Rose Campions, Tea Roses, Mignonette, Marigolds, Coreopsis, the rows of Sweet Peas, the broad-leaved Hollyhocks and the rest, rejoice and grow visibly with every moment of the glorious day. Clematis and Honeysuckle almost seem to hurry, Nasturtiums reach their shield-like leaves and wind the stems thereof round any and every stick and string they can touch by which to lift themselves, here and there showing their first glowing flowers, and climbing eagerly. The long large buds of the white Clematis, the earliest of all, are swelling visibly before my eyes, and the buds of the early June Honeysuckle are reddening at the end of every spray. In one corner a tall purple Columbine hangs its myriad clustered bells; each flower has six shell-like whorls set in a circle, colored like rich amethysts and lined with lustrous silver, white as frost. Cornflowers like living sparks of exquisite color, rose and azure, white and purple, twinkle all over the place, and the heavenly procession begins in good earnest. The Grapevine smooths out its young leaves,— they are woolly and crimson; the wind blows and shows me their grayish-white under surfaces. I think of Browning's tender song, the verse,—

> "The leaf buds on the vine are woolly,
> I noticed that to-day,
> One day more bursts them open fully,
> You know the red turns gray."

The Echinocystus plants that have sprung in thick ranks along the edge of the beds against the piazza are fairly storming up the trellis, having sown themselves in the autumn; they have just really begun to take firm hold, and are climbing hand over hand, as sailors do, with their strong green tendrils stretching out like arms and hands to right and left, laying hold of every available thing by which to cling and spring upward to the very eaves. There in August they form a closely woven curtain of lush, light green, overhung with large, loose clusters of starry white flowers having a pure, delicious fragrance like honey and the wax of the comb.

Now come the most perfect days of the year, blue days, hot on the continent, but heavenly here, where the cool breeze breathes round the islands from the great expanse of whispering water. Delightful it is to lie here and rest and realize all this beauty and rejoice in all its joy! The distant coast-line is dim in soft mirage.

> "Half lost in the liquid azure bloom of a crescent of
> sea,
> The silent, sapphire-spangled, marriage-ring of the
> land."

It lies so lovely, far away! At its edge the water is glassy calm, the houses and large, glimmering piles of buildings along its whole length show white in the hot haze; in the offing the far-off sails are half lost in this shimmering veil; farther out there is a soft wind blowing; little fishing-boats with their sails furled lie at anchor between us and the land, faintly outlined against the delicate tone of the water. All is so still! I hear a bee go blundering into the Bachelor's Buttons that hold up their flowers to the sun like small, compact yellow Roses. Suddenly comes a gush of the song-sparrow's music, but father martin sits at his door very quiet; it is too hot on the red roof of his little house, so he sits at its portal and meditates while his small wife broods within, only now and then from his pretty throat pours a low ripple of sound, melodiously content. I am conscious of the sandpiper calling and the full tide murmuring, and I, too, am content.

47

Outside the garden fence it is as if the flowers had broken their bounds and were rushing down the sloping bank in a torrent of yellow, where the early Artemisias and Eschscholtzias are hastening into bloom, overflowing in a flood of gold that, lightly stirred by every breeze, sends a satin shimmer to the sun. Eschscholtzia—it is an ugly name for a most lovely flower. California Poppy is much better. Down into the sweet plot I go and gather a few of these, bringing them to my little table and sitting down before them the better to admire and adore their beauty. In the slender green glass in which I put them they stand clothed in their delicate splendor. One blossom I take in a loving hand the more closely to examine it, and it breathes a glory of color into sense and spirit which is enough to kindle the dullest imagination. The stems and fine thread-like leaves are smooth and cool gray-green, as if to temper the fire of the blossoms, which are smooth also, unlike almost all other Poppies, that are crumpled past endurance in their close green buds, and make one feel as if they could not wait to break out of the calyx and loosen their petals to the sun, to be soothed into even tranquillity of beauty by the touches of the air. Every cool gray-green leaf is tipped with a tiny line of red, every flower-bud wears a little pale-green pointed cap like an elf, and in the early morning when the bud is ready to blow, it pushes off the pretty cap and unfolds all its loveliness to the sun. Nothing could be more picturesque than this fairy cap, and nothing more charming than to watch the blossom push it off and spread its yellow petals, slowly rounding to the perfect cup. As I hold the flower in my hand and think of trying to describe it, I realize how poor a creature I am, how impotent are words in the presence of such perfection. It is held upright upon a straight and polished stem, its petals curving upward and outward into the cup of light, pure gold with a lustrous satin sheen; a rich orange is painted on the gold, drawn in infinitely fine lines to a point in the centre of the edge of each petal, so that the effect is that of a diamond of flame in a cup of gold. It is not enough that the powdery anthers are orange bordered with gold; they are whirled about the very heart of the flower like a revolving Catherine-wheel of fire. In the centre of the anthers is a shining point of warm sea-green, a last, consummate touch which makes the beauty of the blossom supreme. Another has the orange suffused through the gold evenly, almost to the outer edges of the petals, which are left in bright, light yellow with a dazzling effect. Turning the flower and looking at it from the outside, it has no calyx, but the petals spring from a simple pale-green disk, which must needs be edged with sea-shell pink for the glory of God! The fresh splendor of this flower no tongue nor pen nor brush of mortal man can fitly represent.

Who indeed shall adequately describe any one, the simplest even, of these radiant beings? Day after day, as I watch them appear, one variety after another, in such endless changes of delicate beauty, I can but marvel ever more and more at the exhaustless power of the great Inventor. Must He not enjoy the work of His hands, the manifold perfection of these His matchless creations? Who can behold the unfolding of each new spring and all its blossoms without feeling the renewal of "God's ancient rapture," of which Browning speaks in "Paracelsus"? In that immortal rapture, I, another of His creatures, less obedient in fulfilling His laws of beauty than are these lovely beings, do humbly share, reflecting it with all the powers of my spirit and rejoicing in His work with an exceeding joy.

As the days go on toward July, the earth becomes dry and all the flowers begin to thirst for moisture. Then from the hillside, some warm, still evening, the sweet rain-song of the robin echoes clear, and next day we wake to a dim morning; soft flecks of cloud bar the sun's way, fleecy vapors steal across the sky, the southwest wind blows lightly, rippling the water into little waves that murmur melodiously as they kiss the shore. In this warm gray, brooding light I am reminded of Tennyson's subtle description of such a daybreak:—

> "When the first low matin chirp hath grown
> Full quire, and morning driven her plough of pearl
> Far furrowing into light the mound rack,
> Beyond the fair green field and eastern sea."

Through the early hours of the day the mottled, pearly clouds keep their shape, with delicious open spaces of tempered blue between; by and by the sky's tender fleece is half shadowed, toward noon it melts into loose mists. Color everywhere tells against these pellucid grays,—the gold of Lemon Lilies, the flame of Iceland Poppies, all the sweet tints of every blossom. Presently the happy rain begins to fall, so soft, so warm, so peaceful, the very sound of it is a pleasure; every leaf in the patient garden, which has waited for the shower so long, spreads itself wide to catch each crystal drop and treasure its deep refreshment. All day it rains; at night the melody lulls us to sleep as it patters on the roof. In the night the wind changes, and next day brings a northeast storm again with a wild wind, but from this the little flower plot is well protected, and I rejoice in the thorough watering deep down among their roots which is doing all the plants unmeasured good. Two, perhaps three days, it lasts, the gale blowing till there is such contention of winds and waves about the little isle as to make a ceaseless roaring of wild breakers round its shores. When at last the tempest wears itself out, what delight there is in the great tranquillity that follows it, what music in the soft, far murmurs of ceasing strife in air and ocean, spent wrath that seems to breathe yet in an undertone, half sullen, half relenting, while the broad yellow light that lies over sea and rocks in stillness, like a quiet smile, promises a heavenly day on the morrow.

ALICE MORSE EARLE
(1853–1911)

The old-fashioned garden has always had its charm for Americans, who want to be up to date in so many other ways. Of significance in these old-time gardens are the hedges and walls, which not only form enclosures but also provide a place for ivies and wall plants. Alice Earle's writing is tinged with nostalgia, but it is decidedly unsentimental and very informative.

———————

OLD-TIME GARDENS:
A BOOK OF THE SWEET O' THE YEAR

Garden Boundaries

"A garden fair . . . with Wandis long and small
Railèd about, and so with treès set
Was all the place; and Hawthorne hedges knet,
That lyf was none walking there forbye
That might within scarce any wight espy."
KINGS QUHAIR, KING JAMES I OF SCOTLAND.

One who reads what I have written in these pages of a garden enclosed, will scarcely doubt that to me every garden must have boundaries, definite and high. Three old farm boundaries were of necessity garden boundaries in early days—our stone walls, rail fences, and hedge-rows. The first two seem typically American; the third is an English hedge fashion. Throughout New England the great boulders were blasted to clear the rocky fields; and these, with the smaller loose stones, were gathered into vast stone walls. We still see these walls around fields and as the boundaries of kitchen gardens and farm flower gardens, and delightful walls they are, resourceful of beauty to the inventive gardener. I know one lovely garden in old Narragansett, on a farm which is now the country-seat of folk of great wealth, where the old stone walls are the pride of the place; and the carefully kept garden seems set in a beautiful frame of soft gray stones and flowering vines. These walls would be more beautiful still if

Source: New York: The Macmillan Company, 1901.

52

our climate would let us have the wall gardens of old England, but everything here becomes too dry in summer for wall gardens to flourish.

Rhode Island farmers for two centuries have cleared and sheltered the scanty soil of their state by blasting the ledges, and gathering the great stones of ledge and field into splendid stone walls. Their beauty is a gift to the farmer's descendants in reward for his hours of bitter and wearying toil. One of these fine stone walls, six feet in height, has stood secure and unbroken through a century of upheavals of winter frosts—which it was too broad and firmly built to heed. It stretches from the Post Road in old Narragansett, through field and meadow, and by the side of the oak grove to the very edge of the bay.

. . .

Throughout Narragansett, Locust trees have a fashion of fringing the stone walls with close young growth, and shading them with occasional taller trees.

These form an ideal garden boundary. The stone walls also gather a beautiful growth of Clematis, Brier, wild Peas, and Grapes; but they form a clinging-place for that devil's brood, Poison Ivy, which is so persistent in growth and so difficult to exterminate.

The old worm fence was distinctly American; it had a zig-zag series of chestnut rails, with stakes of twisted cedar saplings which were sometimes "chunked" by moss-covered boulders just peeping from the earth. This worm fence secured to the nature lover and to wild life a strip of land eight or ten feet wide, whereon plant, bird, beast, reptile, and insect flourished and reproduced. It has been, within a few years, a gardening fashion to preserve these old "Virginia" fences on country places of considerable elegance. Planted with Clematis, Honeysuckle, Trumpet vine, Wistaria, and the free-growing new Japanese Roses, they are wonderfully effective.

On Long Island, east of Riverhead, where there are few stones to form stone walls, are curious and picturesque hedge-rows, which are a most interesting and characteristic feature of the landscape, and they are beautiful also, as I have seen them once or twice, at the end of an old garden. These hedge-rows were thus formed: when a field was cleared, a row of young saplings of varied growth, chiefly Oak, Elder, and Ash, was left to form the hedge. These young trees were cut and bent over parallel to the ground, and sometimes interlaced together with dry branches and vines. Each year these trees were lopped, and new sprouts and branches permitted to grow only in the line of the hedge. Soon a tangle of briers and wild vines overgrew and netted them all into a close, impenetrable, luxuriant mass. They were, to use Wordsworth's phrase, "scarcely hedge-rows, but lines of sportive woods run wild." In this close green wall birds build their nests, and in their shelter burrow wild hares, and there open Violets and other firstlings of the spring. The twisted tree trunks in these old hedges are sometimes three or four feet in diameter one way, and a foot or more the other; they were a shiftless field-border, as they took up so much land, but they were sheep-proof. The custom of making a dividing line by a row of bent and polled trees still remains, even where the close, tangled hedge-row has disappeared with the flocks of sheep.

These hedge-rows were an English fashion seen in Hertfordshire and Suffolk. On commons and reclaimed land they took the place of the quickset hedges seen around richer farm lands. The bending and interlacing was called plashing; the polling, shrouding. English farmers and gardeners paid infinite attention to their hedges, both as a protection to their fields and as a means of firewood.

There is something very pleasant in the thought that these English gentlemen who settled eastern Long Island, the Gardiners, Sylvesters, Coxes, and others, retained on their farm lands in the new world the customs of their English homes, pleasanter still to know that their descendants for centuries kept up these homely farm fashions. The old hedge-rows on Long Island are an historical record, a landmark—long may they linger. On some of the finest estates on the island they have been carefully preserved, to form the lower boundary of a garden, where, laid out with a shaded, grassy walk dividing it from the flower beds, they form the loveliest of garden limits. Planted skillfully with great Art to look like great Nature, with edging of Elder and Wild Rose, with native vines and an occasional congenial garden ally, they are truly unique.

Yew was used for the most famous English hedges; and as neither Yew nor Holly thrive here—though both will grow—I fancy that is why we have ever had in comparison so few hedges, and have really no very ancient ones, though in old letters and account books we read of the planting of hedges on fine estates. George Washington tried it, so did [John] Adams, and [Thomas] Jefferson, and [John] Quincy [Adams]. Osage Orange, Barberry, and Privet were in nurserymen's lists, but it has not been till within twenty or thirty years that Privet has become so popular. In Southern gardens, Cypress made close, good garden hedges; and Cedar hedges fifty or sixty years old are seen. Lilac hedges were unsatisfactory, save in isolated cases, as the one at Indian Hill. The Japan Quinces, and other of the Japanese shrubs, were tried in hedges in the mid-century, with doubtful success as hedges, though they form lovely rows of flowering shrubs. Snowballs and Snowberries, Flowering Currant, Altheas, and Locust, all have been used for hedge-planting, so we certainly have tried faithfully enough to have hedges in America. Locust hedges are most graceful, they cannot be clipped closely. I saw one lovely creation of Locust, set with an occasional Rose Acacia—and the Locust thus supported the brittle Acacia. If it were successful, it would be, when in bloom, a dream of beauty. Hemlock hedges are ever fine, as are hemlock trees everywhere, but will not bear too close clipping. Other evergreens, among them the varied Spruces, have been set in hedges, but have not proved satisfactory enough to be much used.

Buckthorn was a century ago much used for hedges and arches. When Josiah Quincy, President of Harvard College, was in Congress in 1809, he obtained from an English gardener, in Georgetown, Buckthorn plants for hedges in his Massachusetts home, which hedges were an object of great beauty for many years.

The traveller Kalm* found Privet hedges in Pennsylvania in 1760. In Scotland Privet is called Primprint. Primet and Primprivet were other old names. Box was called Primpe. These were all derivative of prim, meaning precise. Our Privet hedges, new as they are, are of great beauty and satisfaction, and soon will rival the English Yew hedges.

I have never yet seen the garden in which there was not some boundary or line which could be filled to advantage by a hedge. In garden great or garden small, the hedge should ever have a place. Often a featureless garden, blooming well, yet somehow unattractive, has been completely transformed by the planting of hedges. They seem, too, to give such an orderly aspect to the garden. In level countries hedges are specially valuable. I cannot understand why some denounce clipped hedges and trees as against nature. A clipped hedge is just as natural as the cut grass of a lawn, and is closely akin to it. Others think hedges "too set"; to me their finality is their charm.

* Kalm, Peter (1715–1779). An early plant explorer in America. Linnaeus named the mountain laurel (*Kalmia latifolia*) in his honor.—Ed.

Hedges need to be well kept to be pleasing. Chaucer in his day in praising a "hegge" said that:—

"Every branche and leaf must grow by measure
  Pleine as a bord, of a height by and by."

In England, hedge-clipping has ever been a gardening art.

In the old English garden the topiarist was an important functionary. Besides his clipping shears he had to have what old-time cooks called *judgment* or *faculty*. In English gardens many specimens of topiary work still exist, maintained usually as relics of the past rather than as a modern notion of the beautiful. . . .

In a few old gardens in America, especially in Southern towns, traces of the topiary work of early years can be seen; these overgrown, uncertain shapes have a curious influence, and the sentiment awakened is beautifully described by Gabriele d'Annunzio:—

"We walked among evergreens, among ancient Box trees, Laurels, Myrtles, whose wild age had forgotten its early discipline. In a few places here and there was some trace of the symmetrical shapes carved once upon a time by the gardener's shears, and with a melancholy not unlike his who searches on old tombstones for the effigies of the forgotten dead, I noted carefully among the silent plants those traces of humanity not altogether obliterated."

The height of topiary art in America is reached in the lovely garden, often called the Italian garden, of Hollis H. Hunnewell, Esq., at Wellesley, Massachusetts. Vernon Lee tells in her charming essay on "Italian Gardens" of the beauty of gardens without flowers, and this garden of Mr. Hunnewell is an admirable example. . . . The clear gleam of marble pavilions and balustrades, the formal rows of flower jars with their hundreds of Century plants, and the lovely light on the lovely lake, serve as a delightful contrast to the clear, clean lusty green of the clipped trees. This garden is a beautiful example of the art of the topiarist, not in its grotesque forms, but in the shapes liked by Lord Bacon, pyramids, columns, and "hedges in welts," carefully studied to be both stately and graceful. I first saw this garden thirty years ago; it was interesting then in its well thought-out plan, and in the perfection of every inch of its slow growth; but how much more beautiful now, when the garden's promise is fulfilled.

The editor of *Country Life* says that the most notable attempt at modern topiary work in England is at Ascott, the seat of Mr. Leopold de Rothschild, but the examples there have not attained a growth at all approaching those at Wellesley. Mr. Hunnewell writes thus of his garden:—

"It was after a visit to Elvaston nearly fifty years ago that I conceived the idea of making a collection of trees for topiary work in imitation of what I had witnessed at that celebrated estate. As suitable trees for that purpose could not be obtained at the nurseries in this country, and as the English Yew is not reliable in our New England climate, I was obliged to make the best selection possible from such trees as had proved hardy here—the Pines, Spruces, Hemlocks, Junipers, Arbor-vitæ, Cedars, and Japanese Retinosporas. The trees were all very small, and for the first twenty years their growth was shortened twice annually, causing them to take a close and compact habit, comparing favorably in that respect with the Yew. Many of them are now more than forty feet in height and sixty feet in circumference, the Hemlocks especially proving highly successful."

This beautiful example of art in nature is ever open to visitors, and the number of such visitors is very large. It is, however, but one of the many beauties of the great estate, with its fine garden of Roses, its pavilion of splendid Rhododendrons and Azaleas, its uncommon and very successful rock garden, and its magnificent plantation of rare trees. There are also many rows of fine hedges and arches in various portions of the grounds, hedges of clipped Cedar and Hemlock, many of them twenty feet high, which compare well in condition, symmetry, and extent with the finest English hedges on the finest English estates.

Through the great number of formal gardens laid out within a few years in America, the topiary art has had a certain revival. In California, with the lavish foliage, it may be seen in considerable perfection, though of scant beauty. . . .

Happy is the garden surrounded by a brick wall or with terrace wall of brick. How well every color looks by the side of old brick; even scarlet, bright pink, and rose-pink flowers, which seem impossible, do very well when held to the wall by clear green leaves. Flowering vines are perfect when trained on old soft-red brick enclosing walls; white-flowered vines are specially lovely thereon, Clematis, white Roses, and the rarely beautiful white Wistaria. How lovely is my Virgin's-bower when growing on brick; how Hollyhocks stand up beside it. Brick posts, too, are good in a fence, and, better still, in a pergola. . . .

A very curious garden wall is the serpentine brick wall still standing at the University of Virginia, at Charlottesville. It is about seven feet high, and closes in the garden and green of the row of houses occupied by members of the faculty; originally it may have extended around the entire college grounds. . . . The first thought in the mind of the observer is that its reason for curving is that it could be built much more lightly, and hence more cheaply, than a straight wall; then it seems a possible idealization in brick of the old Virginia rail fence. But I do not look to domestic patterns and influences for its production; it is to me a good example of the old-time domination of French ideas which was so marked and so disquieting in America. In France, after the peace of 1762, the Marquis de Geradin was revolutionizing gardening. His own garden at Ermenonville and his description of it exercised important influence in England and America, as in France. [Thomas] Jefferson was the planner and architect of the University of Virginia; and it is stated that he built this serpentine wall. Whether he did or not, it is another example of French influences in architecture in the United States. This French school, above everything else, replaced straight lines with carefully curving and winding lines.

JOHN McLAREN
(1846–1943)

John McLaren is little known outside of the state of California. Born in Scotland, educated at the Royal Botanic Garden in Edinburgh, as his first job as a landscape gardener he planted sea bent grass to fasten down the dunes near the Firth of Forth. Subsequently, he became superintendent of parks in San Francisco and created Golden Gate Park. His park is of extraordinary arboreal beauty, built on an unpromising site of shifting sand dunes. His advice to the California homeowner is excellent, displaying a kind of thoroughness associated with legendary Scottish gardeners.

GARDENING IN CALIFORNIA
LANDSCAPE AND FLOWER

Planning the Pleasure-Garden and Grounds

The subject of this chapter is one which should receive very careful consideration before the work is actually begun, and a detailed PLAN of planting should be sketched out, especially keeping in view what the effect of the trees, shrubs and plants will be when they reach maturity. What that plan of planting actually may be depends very greatly upon how the ground is located.

If the site selected is on a hill, the character of the planting will be entirely different from that of a location on a level plain, where the situation is more likely to be well sheltered and favored with a deep, rich soil.

In this, as in every work we undertake, the first thing to be considered is the end in view, and the next the best means of attaining that end. As, in the planting of a Pleasure-Garden and Grounds, the end to be attained is how the trees and plants shall be most effectively placed (both that they themselves shall appear to the best advantage and also that each tree and each group of plants and shrubs shall contribute its full proportion to the effective laying out of the property as a whole), in order to attain that end, it is necessary to take advantage of every point in the natural formation of the location.

As has just been stated, the character of the planting on

Source: San Francisco: A. M. Robertson, 1908, 1914.

a hillside site is very different from that on a site located in a sheltered valley. On a hillside site the ground is seldom of an even nature, there frequently being projecting points of land or rocky outcroppings showing through the surface. These projecting points should be ornamented with hardy, strong-growing trees such as the Pine, Eucalyptus, Acacia, Cypress, Redberry and others of this class. No shrub, either exotic or indigenous, is so well adapted to the planting of a rocky ridge or in the foreground of hillside groups as our native Holly (*Heteromeles arbutifolia*). Another native which groups well in any such situation is our evergreen shrub Oak. Like the Redberry, its leaf has a good color, it has a semi-drooping habit of growth, it is evergreen and grows on dry banks on any exposure either North, South, East or West, excepting within a mile from the ocean, where, if facing the West and much exposed, it is apt to get wind-blown and generally does not thrive so well.

Where a shrubbery effect is desired and the soil is rich, some other shrub must be substituted, as the effect of a good soil will be to force the Oak into tree shape and to grow too large for a shrub effect, but where the soil is of a loose, rocky nature, and not too rich, the evergreen native shrub Oak gives one of the best effects possible without cultivation or irrigation.

These hardier trees are recommended also for planting on the outer lines of grounds of the extent of about one acre or over, or on those portions of a Pleasure-Garden which are much exposed or beyond the reach of the hose, and, as already suggested, they can be planted at any parts where the soil is poor.

For the planting of groups or clumps to be located immediately about the lawns or near hydrants where they can be watered, a much larger variety of trees and shrubs may be drawn from, the Bamboo, the Birch, the Maple, the Hawthorn, the Lilac, the Laurel and many others giving character and completeness to the composition.

Where the grounds are as large as from three to four acres, separate groups of each genus should be planted. For instance, exceedingly effective groups can be formed by planting a mass consisting of three or four varieties of Pines; another of Eucalyptus in variety; another of Spruce and Fir, another of a variety of evergreen Oaks; another of our native Laurel; another of Redwood; another of Cedar, and so on; and again, these may be planted so as to form combinations. Such trees as the Maple and Sycamore, or Cedar (Thuya) and Coast Redwood combine beautifully, but it must be particularly kept in view that grouping round-headed trees with those which are of pyramidal habit is a mistake. Round-headed trees must be grouped with those of the same habit, and pyramidal trees with those of similar form, the effect always being pleasing, but mixing those two shapes in the same group mars the effect and ruins the composition.

Evergreens and deciduous trees harmonize very well in a group, provided they are of the same shape and outline. For instance, a group formed by combining the Bamboo with the Birch is most pleasing, both of those being of the same graceful semi-pendulous habit.

It should, then, be remembered, in massing groups of trees for planting, that form and habit should be studied much more closely than any other quality.

In planning the groups it may be found desirable and effective to form some entirely of evergreens, others entirely of deciduous trees and shrubs, and others of a mixture of both, a very good combination being a group of our native Laurel and the European Linden, because both are of the same graceful habit of growth.

The same rule applies to the planting of shrubbery masses; the stiff and the formal should never be associated with the rounded, free-spreading kinds—that is, the kinds whose limbs spread wide and rest gracefully on the surface of the lawn.

In the disposition of a number of sorts of trees and shrubs in the landscape, the same principle must be followed in producing variety and harmony. If they are mixed together in a haphazard way, the results will very rarely be pleasing, but, at the same time, monotony must be guarded against. For example, groups of Oaks should not be followed by groups of round-headed trees, but rather by a mass formed of such trees as the California Laurel, while next to the Laurel might come the Poplar or some other tree of similar column-shaped head and symmetry. Then again, when groups meet, they might sometimes be blended together. For example, a group of Oaks, adjoining a group of California Laurels, might be blended into the Laurel group, by the Oaks being planted so as to overlap the Laurels and the Laurels the Oaks, as is to be found in natural groups.

The same rule applies to shrubs and even to flowers at the extreme points of the groups.

When a group of Pines adjoins a group of Live Oaks, it is always desirable to blend the two groups at the junction of the one with the other, care being taken to avoid regular progression and everything like formality, and it being borne in mind that grounds laid out according to simple plans are generally much more pleasing than those laid out on over-pretentious lines.

Neltje Blanchan
(1865–1918)

*How practical and how refreshingly American Neltje
Blanchan is! Her ideas on relating of the American flower
garden to the American landscape and to the specific site in
the landscape are good ones and thoughtfully given. This
advice was written at the time when the Italianate garden,
encouraged by Edith Wharton and Charles Platt, was all the
rage. To the contrary, she offers no "style" as more important
than another, but instead encourages individuality in the
making of gardens. How American! How likely to
be found again in 1994!*

———————

The American Flower Garden

Situation and Design

One reason why English gardens are so wonderful to us Americans is that successive generations, perhaps for hundreds of years, have been lovingly and intelligently at work upon them, each striving to adorn the main design in some new detail before passing over the inheritance to the next heir. At the sight of the surpassing beauty of Old World country estates, as contrasted with our raw, new, mushroom homes, that are rarely lived in by two generations, one is almost persuaded against his better judgment that inheritance through primogeniture and entail must be the proper method. Perhaps we may be wise enough some day to achieve the same ends by more just means, consistent with republican, not monarchic, conditions. Instead of endowing our oldest sons, the heirs-apparent to our little thrones, we may endow the homestead itself—who knows!—just as we endow hospitals and colleges to insure their future maintenance. Happy the children who are brought up in a little world of beauty and who may one day hope to inherit it all—the well grown trees, the velvety lawn, the established vines and shrubbery—all the cumulative results of love's labor. Certainly, unless one may work for permanence in the garden there can be little incentive in this country toward the best art out-of-doors.

It is, of course, expecting too much that the site of the house should be chosen solely with reference to the best con-

Source: New York: Doubleday, Page & Company, 1909.

ditions for its garden. We place our homes, as a general rule, not where there is good, rich loam, not where fine trees are already established and the situation is sheltered, but where the house will be convenient to the railroad station, the school, our friends, or the golf links; or where a special bargain in real estate may be had, or where the greatest number of windows will command the finest views, or where the prevailing summer breezes will sweep through the living-rooms, or where they will be protected from winter winds, or where the sunshine may pour health into them, or where perfect drainage and a water supply are best assured. These and a hundred other practical reasons may dominate the selection of a building site. Relying upon the bounty of nature to provide embellishments for every spot on earth man has yet decided to live upon—and she has plants for every place and purpose—we have been too apt to ignore the garden's claims until the eleventh hour and to concentrate all our thought, oftentimes all of our money plus a mortgage, upon the house itself, leaving little or nothing for the setting of the home picture, in which, after all, the house should be merely the most important detail.

But if there is to be a union of the house and the landscape into which it obtrudes—a happy marriage between the house and the garden—the help of the artist-gardener is needed most of all before the house is started, I had almost said before the land is bought. For it is the design of a place as a whole that is the main thing, whether the size of the picture that is to be wrought out is reckoned in miles, acres, or square feet. If the home-maker cannot afford to execute the whole plan at the outset, it is all the more reason that he should possess such a design and proceed methodically to do what he can, year by year, to execute it permanently, rather than waste his money on costly experiments. A rich man can afford mistakes; a poor one cannot. Moving soil, for example, is surprisingly expensive. A cart-load of it dumped on a

lawn looks but little larger than an ant-hill, and the equiva-
lent of a landscape architect's fee might be easily wasted in an
unintelligent disposal of the top soil alone. A plan which
involves annual upheavals and repeated efforts upon the
same piece of land and the incessant care of a skilled gardener, is a very poor plan indeed for a man of modest means.
Skyrocket effects of coleus, geraniums and other bedding
plants from the florist are rarely desirable in any case, but
usually the novice's first undirected efforts are to get them.
All plants require some attention, but not necessarily annual
attention; certainly not annual renewal. A permanent planting of hard shrubs and perennials has all the artistic qualities
and the practical ones as well. Since it takes years for newly
planted trees to look thoroughly at home, delay in setting
them out means a needless prolonging of the raw, unfinished
state of the place. The era of vanity—or was it parsimony?—
when every man presumed to be his own lawyer, his own
doctor, or architect, or garden designer, is happily being
superseded by an age of specialists whom the wise consult
more and more.

It goes without saying that the professional gardener to
be chosen should be practical as well as an artist—one who
has had too much experience with growing things to advise
planting elms on a dry, sandy hill-top or tea roses near Que-
bec. Enormous sums have been wasted on rhododendrons
alone, through attempting to grow in this country imported
foreign hybrids which soon give up the struggle for existence
in our uncongenial climate; whereas lasting and equally beautiful effects may be produced from hardy hybrids of our
native rhododendron race. Costly mistakes are made annually in planting yews and certain other European evergreens.
Manchuria and Siberia, with climatic conditions similar to
our own, are likely to yield far more valuable treasures for
the lawn and garden than the continent of Europe, where we
have looked too long, not only for models of design, which

may be sometimes desirable, but for the plants to execute them, which most often are not.

Where is that nurseryman's catalogue so frankly honest that the novice may learn from it what *not* to buy? It is safe to say that millions of dollars [sic] worth of plants die for the lack of intelligent selection, planting, or care. Decidedly, for economic reasons as well as artistic, we Americans are sorely in need of more disinterested, expert advice. But beware of the adviser who has an axe to grind. There are some excellent men connected with nursery establishments of the highest class, but the frequent tendency is to retain "landscape gardeners" of little or no artistic training whose real business is to sell plants for their employers. Naturally the temptation is to load the client with as much stock as possible, regardless of its value to the general effect of his place. "Plant thick; thin quick," is a popular saying in the trade. The disinterested professional, with no commercial connections, makes it his business to secure for his client the best stock that may be purchased anywhere in the open market and at the lowest price. Likewise beware of the landscape gardener who does not insist upon studying the garden problem on the land where it is to be worked out; who would attempt to furnish a design from a few photographs of your grounds at his office desk, or copy another garden that he made successfully elsewhere. Ninety-nine chances out of one hundred it will not suit your place; perhaps not a single feature could be transferred to advantage. It is easier to copy than to originate, but rarely satisfying either to the æsthetic or to the moral sense.

The architect of the house, who very often essays the rôle of designer of its surroundings, that the effect of his work may not be spoiled by his client, usually lacks a knowledge of plants, without which there can be no lasting success. Such knowledge can be had only by years of special study and experiment, quite beyond the attainment of most professional architects. The landscape gardener on the other hand, very often lacks the needful knowledge of design, apart from the naturalistic treatment of very large parklike areas. He may know a great deal about plants, how to choose and how to grow them, but usually he knows very little about the principles of art and design, or how to treat the land adjoining buildings. The natural landscape he understands, and his usual endeavour is to bring its purely informal lines right up to the purely formal lines of a building, with disastrous results from the artistic view-point. Happily there are not a few well-rounded men, however, trained in design as well as horticulture, who are lifting the art of gardening in this country to a higher plane than it ever before attained here. And more will be forthcoming when their value is more generally appreciated.

But if, for any sufficient cause, one may not employ disinterested, expert advice, one may at least proceed in the artistic spirit along reasonable lines, acquiring by patient study of one's own peculiar problem the knowledge necessary to solve it, and so enjoy one's self all the fun of garden making. Then, indeed, the garden becomes one's very own and best beloved. It is not, or should not be, a matter of capricious taste, but a matter of reason and the affections. Principles of composition govern its making, it is true, as surely as they do a painting in oils; nevertheless the application of those principles to each individual garden problem should be as various as the gardens themselves that each may possess its own distinctive features and charm. Personality reflected in a garden may be its chief attraction. Better a craving for the ideal carried to a "fine lunacy" than the coldly correct, impersonal art of an unimpassioned hireling. It were happiness indeed if, when the time for garden making comes, Art

"shall say to thee:
'I find you worthy, do this thing for me.'"

Before daring to proceed with a single detail on the place, study your piece of land as a whole from every point of view. Map it out on a large sheet of tough paper. Draw it to scale, if possible. Show its elevations and depressions and respect these as far as may be when you come to grade rather than attempt the expense and achieve the ugliness of reducing the land to a monotonous level like a billiard table. Every plot of ground, like every human face, has an individuality to be emphasised rather than obliterated. If your place is not a small one, divide the map into several enlarged sections for special study and treatment. This book can help you with only one section, the area to be pictorially treated. It concerns itself with the flower garden only, not with forestry, road-making, the vegetable garden, orchard, vineyard, poultry yard, or any other utilitarian subject, however important, that may engage the home-maker's attention. But the flower garden, of many types, is broadly interpreted to include the lawn and the trees and shrubs suitable for it, because these contribute so immeasurably to the garden picture that no really good one can be made without them. . . .

On the chart of the garden area put arrows to indicate the directing of objects of beauty or interest, such as a fine view, a vista through the trees, a gigantic pine, or a mirror-like lake toward which attention should be directed. Put crosses where unsightly objects need to be screened or planted out; but first make very sure that what you have considered an eye-sore may not be transformed into an object of beauty. Consider deepening the dismal swamp into a pond for a water garden; covering the dead tree with a mantle of vines instead of chopping it down; making an alpine garden among the rocks instead of blasting them out.

Think well before locating the house, even on paper, and include the drive or path by which it is to be approached in your calculations. Many a house has been completed before it was discovered that the only route left to it approached from the worst possible point of vantage, or spoiled the chances for a good broad lawn, or necessitated too steep a grade, or cut the garden picture in half.

Oftentimes considerable planting may be done on larger grounds than suburban lots before the house is built, but only on the area outside of the building operations, where the carpenter's, plumber's and painter's horses will not feast upon the tender new growth or strip off the bark from your favourite possessions. As soon as the design of your place has been mapped out, a list of such trees, shrubs and hardy perennials as will be needed to execute it may be made. Do not try to collect a museum of plants; avoid freaks of variegated foliage, exclamation points of colour, strange exotics that look out of place in our American landscape, and the beguiling novelties of the catalogues. Personally visit several reliable nurseries if possible, making your own selections and see them tagged with your name. Choose well-grown, vigorous stock at a fair price rather than the puny disappointments that, alas! are what tempt so many because they are erroneously considered cheap. Many a man, intensely practical in his own business, will give his order to the lowest bidder among competing nurserymen and waste years looking at sickly, struggling or dying trees, shrubs and perennials about his home rather than invest a little more money and get satisfaction and joy from the start. Poor stock is dear at any price.

In an out-of-the-way corner of your place prepare the ground for a little nursery of your own by deeply ploughing the soil, enriching it well, and lightening it, if it be heavy, with sand, leaf-mould from the woods or humus from the compost heap. Plants make very slow growth in clay soil. A rich, sandy loam, cool and moist with much decomposed vegetable matter through it, favours the rapid growth that the owner of a new place so greatly longs for. As soon as the stock arrives, set it out in rows, with room to spread and with sufficient space between the rows for cultivation with the wheeled hoe. A mulch of stable litter or leaves will protect the roots from drying out in summer and from winter frosts. Perhaps a greater percentage of nursery stock dies for the lack of mulching before it becomes well established than from any other cause. If the house is not to be built for a few years, this little nursery will yield a very high rate of compound interest, for the small stock, which it pays the nurseryman best to sell you, was comparatively cheap, but it would be sadly ineffective on a new place; whereas the larger, older stock you now possess, which is disproportionately costly and difficult to buy, gives delightful, quick results. Be sure you know just the tree or shrub for a given spot on your place before buying it. One can no more plant one's grounds in a hurry than one can successfully furnish a house outright in a week. One must feel one's way along, and realise the need of a certain plant for a certain place before proceeding to get it.

Near the place chosen for the garden, its jealous guardian angel will save every precious ounce of top soil and sod that comes from the site of the house and the cutting of drives and paths. There will be no wasteful burning of leaves in the autumn. What are not needed as a mulch will form the basis of a rich compost heap piled up with broken sod, cut grass, manure, and wood ashes. The merest novice must know that there can be no success in a garden without a careful study of the soil, and the needs of the various species of plants that are to draw their sustenance from it.

Some situations there are, a very few, where a house may be placed in the midst of wild scenery, so surpassingly beautiful in itself, that any garden artifice attempted seems a profanation. But even a camp in the wildest Adirondacks, without some planting about it to simulate Nature's garden coming to its very doors, appears to spring impertinently from the soil like a Jack-from-the-box. The very act of building a house anywhere destroys nature's balance, and man's best endeavours are required first of all to restore harmony. Whether the situation demands a wild garden or a formal one, the matter of fundamental importance is to establish the right relationship at the outset between the house and its environment.

A bit of wild tangled woodland is very beautiful, but it is not a garden, and the moment a man thrusts a spade into the earth or fells a tree, or sets out a plant where one did not grow before, that moment he becomes responsible for the effect of the land he subverts to his will. A garden should be "man's report of earth at her best."

There are those ardent lovers of unspoiled nature who consider any house a pimple on her face. Salve it over with vines, veil it heavily with trees and shrubbery, still it is a blemish to be apologized for, if not concealed. Surely a well-designed house, pure in style and restrained in treatment, needs no apology for its existence. Beauty of architecture is its own excuse for being. In this day of well-trained architects there should be no excuse, except the untrained client, for building an ugly house. Unhappily, mongrel architecture is still in our midst— "the pug-Newfoundland-poodle-hound-style," a famous architect calls it—but it is passing, and a distinguished Englishman who recently revisited this country after an absence of fifteen years declares that in no direction have the Americans made more rapid advance than in the building of beautiful homes. We have learned the wisdom of consulting the best architects before attempting to build. As a people, we have not yet learned to seek advice of a similar artistic grade when it comes to the treatment of that most important piece of land in all the world—the area, be it large or small, around the home; which is why one may see a dozen good houses before one can discover a single beautiful, satisfying bit of art out-of-doors. Every architect, let us hope, will one day have a professional gardener associate in his office. Their work is largely interdependent. The advantage of frequent conferences between them would be immeasurable to the client.

The style of architecture best adapted to the climate, natural situation and purse of the owner having been decided, the next problem to present itself is how to tie the bald new house to the landscape into which it suddenly obtrudes. Obviously the solution must vary in every case. The Colonial type of house would lose its dignity if surrounded by woods and a wild garden like a log camp, and the unpretentious little seaside vacation cottage be made ridiculous by an Italian garden on a terrace. A Spanish house needs palms, yuccas and other tropical or semi-tropical garden accessories under Southern skies. Each style of architecture and no style of architecture demand a different setting. While the stately, perfectly proportioned Georgian type requires a formal, balanced treatment of trees and shrubbery masses immediately about it, and implies the box-edged parterres filled with old-fashioned flowers as a central feature of the garden design, the house of nondescript architecture, which might well be called the Predominant, may be treated electively, and sometimes most informally. Even the house that is "Queen Anne in front and Mary Ann behind" may have some of its ugliness mercifully concealed. It is a mistake to suppose that design can concern formality only. Where the architecture is not pure, vines, shrubbery and trees, judiciously placed, may perhaps conceal the defects, which is one of the many things to be said in favour of the informal treatment. Although such a house may have shrubs and flowers all about it, it may possess no special spot that might properly be called a flower garden at all. However, there are very few houses indeed that are not improved by a formal touch about them somewhere. Most houses, of whatever style, are benefited through carrying the principles of architectural design out to their immediate surroundings. Not every Elizabethan house was set on a bowling green above a hedged and knotted garden, nor need it be to-day; but surely no one with the artistic spirit would try to unite it to the landscape by a Japanese garden. Yet a newly rich lady, whose architect had achieved a Tudor triumph in stone and half timber, surrounded it with a poor imitation of a Japanese landscape in miniature within six weeks after the architect's back was turned.

"I can never forgive you," wrote the enraged designer.

"What concern is it of yours? Isn't your bill paid?" replied the complacent parvenu, who, that very day, was arranging for the Japanese water-garden of many storks, stones and bridges to be fed from an old Florentine fountain on the other side of the house. The idea of giving her Elizabethan house a suitable setting in which the shades of Lord Bacon or Shakespeare himself might feel at home, could not enter such a head unaided by a tactful professional gardener.

The style of architecture of the house may be a limitation or a great opportunity, whichever one is pleased to consider it. Infinite variety is possible with the historic method. It is not necessarily stereotyped.

There are cases, perhaps, where a better architectural effect may be had by bringing an unbroken stretch of lawn to the very foundations of a house where vines and fringe of shrubbery might be their only screen; but in order that it may give the most pleasure, the garden should be conveniently near the dwelling. Then it may be lived with and lived in, enjoyed without effort, seen from the windows by busy workers indoors, tended with the least trouble, quickly robbed of some of its wealth for vases by the mistress of the house, its interests safeguarded by every member of the family, as well as the hired man. Only by living with one's garden can its beauties be fully realised, for every passing cloud changes the effect of light and atmosphere—the most potent factors of beauty out-of-doors. A garden by moonlight becomes a new revelation. Then every defect is concealed, glaring colors recede into nothingness, and only the white flowers—the long fragrant trumpets of nicotine, spires of foxgloves, tall white lilies, a Milky Way of cosmos stars, snow balls of phlox and peonies or a foam of boltonia—have their loveliness enhanced by the night.

If we must walk through wet grass to a distant part of the grounds on a hot day, perhaps to an end of the vegetable garden devoted to flowers, before the eyes may feast upon them, or a few blossoms may be gathered for the dinner table, immeasurable pleasure is lost, as well as a decorative adjunct to the house. What would the little cottages of England look like without the gay gardens around every doorstep? How much a well composed garden may add to the beauty of the house itself by extending lines that end too abruptly, by softening sharp angles, by broadening the effect of a house that is too high for its width with masses of shrubbery or hedges on its sides, by nestling around a house on a hill top, or by reconciling another to a plain! The house and garden should seem to be inseparable complements each of the other.

It is conceivable, however, that not every desirable building site would permit a garden near the dwelling, that is, not a garden of definite boundaries. A cottage perched on a cliff overhanging the sea, for example, could not have flower beds and specimen trees and shrubs on the rocky ledges, nor would they be desirable; but the storm-resisting native pines and hardy stunted shrubbery—bayberry, barberries, St. John's wort and broom—would grow there and perfectly fit the landscape. A tide of flowers might surge around the rocky base of the promontory, and some flotsam and jetsam of bloom, like the sand-loving portulacca and sea-pinks, extend almost to the waves. Where nature left off and art began it would be impossible for any one but the maker of that garden to say. Every region has its own wealth of native plants which should be drawn from much more freely than it is. The laurel was quite without honour in its own country until after it had become a favourite in Europe, thanks to its introduction by Peter Kalm, when we could actually import it from European nurseries more conveniently than we could dig it from the woods at home.

A garden is no less a garden because it defies all limitations and conventions. And the artistic spirit likewise refuses to be bound by the fads and fancies of the gardener's craft. Art out-of-doors is universal, like nature herself, and knows no predilection for Italian gardens above wild gardens, for informal or naturalistic ones rather than for the prim, box-edged flower beds of our grandmothers, for the water garden in the humid East above the cactus garden of the desert. Fitness and beauty suffice. Happily every garden site is a law unto itself to which the gardener must submit. No two gardens, no two human faces, were ever alike. Both have individuality as their chief charm.

But it is generally conceded that every garden picture is improved by a frame. The sea, a wood, a tree-girt lawn, a lake, a hedge, a wall, a court yard, a pergola, a terrace, a hillside, or the house itself, any or several of these, and some other boundaries, natural and artificial, may set off the garden's own peculiar beauty to the best advantage. The needs of plants are so various that their loveliness can best be shown in a variety of situations and settings.

GRACE TABOR
(ca. 1872–ca. 1972)

*There are garden styles to match house styles, and Grace
Tabor skillfully threads her way through these design
difficulties. She believes in the power of architecture and
equally in the necessity of the garden to reinforce the whole.
Enclosure is still seen by her as of supreme importance—that
is, enclosure by means of high walls. Yet it was at this time
that gardens were becoming more open, and privacy from
the prying eyes of neighbors was considered
a bit old-fashioned.*

OLD-FASHIONED GARDENING
A HISTORY AND A RECONSTRUCTION

Design

Every individual is so constituted that he has an inherent preference for certain things; just as each has his own peculiar and individual personality, stamped from within, in color and form, upon the body which his fellows see and know. And this strongly marked, inherent preference for the thing admired, along with an equally strong prejudice against the thing unfavored, shared by all of us, makes counsel of a certain sort almost certainly futile. All of which I think is particularly true of ourselves as Americans; we know what we like, each one of us—and we know it *hard*. That there may happen to be flocks of sheep minds going *en masse* in this or that direction, or that the direction in which any given flock is traveling frequently changes, does not lessen the fact that our preferences are decided and distinctly formed—and that we are well aware of them.

So among the five classes into which the old garden designs range themselves, each of us will probably find himself or herself altogether out of sympathy with four, and quite involuntarily prepared to take sides with the fifth. Spanish warrior, English adventurer, Dutch burgher, Puritan reformer, and peaceful Quaker, all made their gardens in this fair and fragrant land within the same century; and the hand of each writ large upon the earth its signature. Which will you have?

Source: New York: McBride, Nast & Company, 1913.

Which is the best—which offers most? These, of a certainty, are the instant demand; but be not deceived. Your final choice is not going to be determined by the answers, even though the questions are deliberated over and well weighed, and a scrupulous, judicial attitude is maintained. No indeed; it is something within that has already leaped and claimed its own, even as the deliberating and weighing are going on, which decides the matter. Deep in the heart of hearts of every one of us there is this correspondence with our own which nothing can shatter; and all choosing against it, let me say in passing, is wrong choosing, be the choice never so plausible and well intentioned. "Which is best?" means therefore, which is best for the asker; "which offers most?" which offers most to him who has raised the query.

Taken in the largest sense, design—as applied to an estate and gardens—means simply plan, refined and perfected until it expresses beauty as well as convenience. Certain underlying and obvious principles of convenience are of course common to all design—that is, to plan, in its primitive simplicity. These principles form foundation lines, or what among professional designers would be called the skeleton of the pattern. And every pattern must have them. Indeed they are so important to it that even in the most intricate and seemingly difficult finished product, the trained designer can trace these skeletons; and the total number of them which it is possible to frame is astonishingly low. So in the garden's pattern they are not many, we may be sure.

In the older design there was no thought of elaborating upon them. Childish simplicity pervades the ancient Spanish garden; it speaks eloquently in the almost total lack of any form except the obvious one which the boundaries of the place suggest, as also in the naïve variations in divisions that are intended to be uniform. There is an uncompromising brusqueness in divisional lines, too, which is childlike. And the attitude of irresponsibility, carelessness, indifference and indolence which was responsible for the untidy condition so characteristic of Spanish gardens, is similarly childlike. Nature was prodigal, as the Spaniard knew her—so why should man be careful? To-morrow, to-morrow—even as little children procrastinate—always to-morrow!

Once the fantastic mosaic pavement of the vari-colored stones was laid along his walks and in the court before his door, little was needed to keep them clean for his enjoyment. The rain would wash them and the wind would sweep them dry—and if a grassy tuft ventured here or there, what harm? Or if a weed or two or three came to dwell among the flowers? Were there not plenty of the latter? And who should keep the roses that had faded plucked and tidy, when roses were forever blooming and fading? Enough that the box-wood was kept true to its purpose; the rest was as fair and as heavy with rich fragrance under comfortable negligence, as the most distressing labors would avail to make it.

Coming north to Virginia the very opposite is found, with Col. Fitzhugh's estate and its quite imposing array of buildings—five he mentions, besides the dwelling-house, and does not include the "quarters" of the immediate family servants—as an example of a less ingenuous style of living. This, with its garden "a hundred foot square" is the earliest model we have of the English gentleman's garden in America. It was made before the simple and sensible Elizabethan designs had been dwarfed by the work of Le Nôtre; for Versailles was only in process of construction about the time Col. Fitzhugh set out his orchard, probably.

His description does not give any hint, unhappily, of the relative positions occupied by his dwelling, the outhouses and his gardens, except that he says the houses are in a "Yeard . . . pallizado'd with locust Puncheons." This proves very certainly, however, that they did not occupy the position or positions, which were later assigned to these buildings—that is, at the right and left of the house. The garden dimensions were too limited for a kitchen garden for such a household as his; and this fact, together with the form of it—a square—which was the form commonly adopted in the Elizabethan designs to balance the house, affords pretty conclusive warrant for the assumption that it was, in the more advanced sense, a "garden." If it were, it would be likely to lay before the dwelling, at the back probably—that is, on the side opposite the main entrance. Perhaps the orchard was beyond, but that is speculation; so also is any attempt to locate the offices.

The counsel of William Lawson doubtless served many of these early southern planters. He suggests much that is delightful in his "New Orchard and Garden," of which some copies of the 1626 edition must certainly have found their way to America and been frequently consulted. He does not say much about design, however; most of his work is horticultural and only generally descriptive of what should or may be done for the greatest pleasure. Genuinely did he love Nature, his especial delight being the orchard; of this he writes with great tenderness and feeling, always. Here in one place, it "takes away the tediousnesse and heavie load of three or four score years!" Again it "is the honest delight of one wearied with the workes of his lawful calling." Everywhere he dwells upon its beauty and charm quite as much as he dwells upon its importance and great value, economically; yet he is a decidedly practical writer who always advises wisely and for efficiency.

Fifty years later another book about garden making came out in England—a huge affair—which must also have interested the garden-making gentry here. This gave some quite detailed directions, and many designs, some of which are shown. The fruit garden or orchard "of forty square yards"—meaning of course forty yards square—with a flower garden half that size, is pronounced sufficient for a "private gentleman"; a nobleman may enlarge upon these so that he has eighty yards square for his fruit, and thirty for his flower garden. A wall of brick all around, nine feet high, with a five-foot wall dividing the fruits from the flowers, shows that he expects these two to join. Large square beds in the flower gardens were to be railed with painted wooden rails or bordered with box "or palisades for dwarf trees"—low pales for cordons probably.

Nearly all his gardens are squares, with beds shaped to fit along walls and into the corners. This gives to many of them the L form, to some the T. He suggests the middle of one side of the flower garden as a suitable site for a summerhouse, which shall serve also as a countinghouse for the garden's wealth of precious bulbs when these are dug for storing. He insists upon a hotbed and a "Nursery"—but does not say where they shall be put.

Dutch influence was so strong in all garden design, in every part of the world, at this time, that there seems very little to say of the Dutch as a separate class of designers. Squares on squares, squares in squares, and squares ranged around a circle—these are the basis of the Dutch designs. Elongated sometimes to an oblong form they are, when the circle is drawn out also into an oval; but curiously enough, this is done only on the vertical axis—on the straightaway from the view point—being intended to overcome perspective and create the illusion of a perfect square and circle! The foreshortening of a square narrows it of course to a seemingly oblong form, lying broadside to the observer. If the dimension which is thus seemingly diminished is actually lengthened just the right amount, the laws of perspective present it to the eye as equal to the actual length of the horizontal dimension; and thus the Dutchman's beloved square and circle are preserved to his critical and exact eye without a flaw.

In New England, as we have already seen, there was very little attempt at garden making. They "gardened" but made no permanent gardens. In so far as there was design, however, it embodied what had been learned from the Dutch during the sojourn in Holland. A few of the little front yards had a little square bed on either side of the walk which led up to the front door; a very few others that were larger had on each side of this walk a border, perhaps, with a bed beyond—or four little square beds, centred on a little round bed in the middle, all very tiny and choking with the boxwood as it grew. Larger grounds were planned and planted practically as grounds are to-day—that is, as it happened. New England had and has lovely gardens, but the earliest offer nothing original nor very interesting.

Finally there were the Quakers, with their long, restful horizontal lines repeated everywhere. Pennsbury gives a striking example of these in the three long rows of walnuts running across the front, down near the river; in the long house—sixty feet it extended—with the forty-foot court at the end, and then beyond this the long group of offices. Altogether the line of buildings must have extended quite two hundred feet or more; for house and court were a hundred, then brew- and malt-house fifty-five—its shorter dimension may have been on the building line, though I doubt it, for this would have made it extend beyond the house towards the back; but even this is thirty-five feet—then the barn, carriage-house, tool-house, poultry-house and all the rest.

Remember that Penn especially stipulated that all should be uniform and not "a scu" from the house; and the description mentions particularly that the offices were "arranged alongside on the front line of it." In this wonderful expanse

there was only one break—the space occupied by the court—
and here the row of English redheart cherry trees continued
the line, and gave continuity to a group which must have
conveyed a sense of comfort and rest and *home* quite without
parallel.

Which of all these *is* the best? Each must answer for
himself. Designing a garden to-day along any one of these
five lines is a simple enough task, once the selection is made.
That selection, as I have tried to show, is the crucial thing;
and altogether a personal matter. Some of the considerations
which might influence it, outside of personal taste—indeed,
which should influence it, regardless of personal taste—are,
first of all, the system of buildings to be erected, or already
erected. I speak of them as a system because that is what they
were in the old times, distinctly; and in more than one section
during the era with which we are dealing.

The house was of course the most important thing in a
system, in one way—the keynote, so to speak—but every
building had its use and was a necessary part of the industrial
life of which the house was the center and the object. Unless
the requirements of an estate are such, therefore, that a
group system is convenient and practical, it is hardly necessary for me to say that any old garden design which has been
developed as a result of such a system, is inappropriate. The
choice of an old design is not merely a choice of a shape for
a flower garden; it is a choice which must consider the entire
place and be governed by the conditions prevailing, which
will continue to prevail.

All farms may be said to require the group system of
buildings. The old Dutch *bouweries* with their helter-skelter
placing of the offices, yet with the garden still rigidly exact in
position and design, afford one treatment of this requirement; the stately plantations of Virginia, whereon the great
house stands in fine dignity flanked by its two groups of

dependent serving-houses, deal with it in another way; while the models of the middle ground, with dwelling and offices ranged on either side of a level court, or on either side of a long and usually low connecting wing that makes them into one building, show still another. All three are distinctly different and offer variety to suit nearly every taste. But if it is not enough, there is New England to fall back upon, with her farmhouses of far-extending kitchen wings, strung out sometimes behind, sometimes at the side, but always along the way that led to the far distant, single, huge building which combined stable, storehouse, workshop and practically all the rest under the comprehensive term of "barn." This use of a "barn"—common now though it is in the greater part of the country—is so different from the undoubtedly wiser provision of older races that even the dictionary takes note of its singularity, saying: "In the United States a part of the barn is often used for stable." Actually a barn is a covered, closed-in place for storage, and never a shelter or dwelling for livestock.

The city plan of William Penn, with its stipulation that each house shall stand in the middle, breadthwise, of its plot, carries no suggestion of outside offices, neither do the accounts of New Amsterdam nor of Massachusetts Bay. But these all have to do with towns; and dwellers in the town, with none of the wide range of domestic activities which the little world of a plantation supported, would have no use for the many office buildings of the great county seat. A stall for a cow, one for a horse possibly, a small carriage shelter, and quarters for barndoor fowl, would meet the needs of the small town residence, then as now. And in the restricted area of a town plot, the country dweller's desire for a compactness which meant convenience, was superseded by the wish to expand as far as possible—to leave as much land about the house free and unobstructed as might be, and to remove the odors of the stable yard to as great a distance from the house as the size of the plot would permit.

Hence we have the house at one end—right on the street line usually—with the outbuildings, under one roof very often, at the extreme other end. If there was a garden or small family orchard, it of course lay between. This is the arrangement which we usually see now; in only one respect in fact have our present towns and suburban districts altered this earliest plan—and this change is not a change in plan, in the sense of design. But in the old days the garden wall was an essential part of the scheme, north, south and between. No one would have thought of omitting it, any more than he would have thought of omitting the bolts on his front door. Within this wall lay the individual's own world, a place whose boundaries were jealously marked and guarded. Public highways harbored very real dangers long after the wilderness beyond the town had ceased to be wilderness; a high and sturdy wall was an actual protection, therefore, and from much more than prying eyes.

Back of this wall might lie the precise and regular garden of a Dutchman, or the long simple flat lines that bespoke the Quaker; or the happen-so of planting which prevailed in New England. But in any event *there was the wall*, six to nine feet high; and straight around the domain it went, from house corner at one side to house corner at the other, the house itself completing the defense.

Looking back to-day, with our suburban acres of barren open "front lawns," and our gardenless settlements for comparison, I am impelled to the belief that this wall was the chief factor in the charm of the smaller old, old gardens. Not every one will agree with me; and of many who agree, few will wish to risk the criticism which such innovation and implied reserve, in the midst of to-day's suburban frankness, would subject them to. But for those who dare, the reward within the walls is great and sure, and not long deferred.

Whether it is better to employ the old garden as only a suggestion for the new, or whether it shall serve as a model, to be duplicated with faithful exactness, is a question into the solution of which many considerations will enter. There is no reason against reproducing an old design, providing every phase of it receives proper attention and no anachronism is permitted. An old garden design built around a modern house, however—that is, a house of modern style—would belittle both old and new; and there is really no reason for ever perpetrating anything so unpleasant.

The primary and only reason that there can be for restoring the old type of garden is either a genuinely old house, or a modern house designed and constructed on the old lines. Architects offer us the distinctly New England Colonial, the Dutch Colonial, the Georgian house of the South—as well as the Southern Colonial—and an interesting type associated with that section which I have called the "Divide." And besides these, there is the Mission or plastered, semi-Moorish house of the far South.

For each of these, there is a garden distinctly its own; and as a matter of fact, no other type of garden can be adjusted to it with any degree of satisfaction. This is the penalty which the revival of a style exacts—a bondage into which it is very easy to deliver oneself unwittingly and innocently sometimes, to repent of most bitterly. Do not enter here unless it will be no burden to submit and see it through.

Old gardens constantly furnish us with suggestions, of course, and have been doing so since they themselves were new; so there is little to be said in regard to this use of them. That it would be well if the simplicity of them acted as a restraint on the tendency to over-elaborate designs, from which we suffer, is perhaps one point that cannot be too persistently emphasized. A student of garden design cannot fail to be struck with the anxiety for novelty and the restlessness which pervades much of the modern work; and some of the great gardens of recent years are oppressive in their over-elaboration and intricacy. This is to be expected, of course, in an age like the present; but it is nevertheless lamentable. For a garden should breathe rest and refreshment, and furnish a retreat for nervous activity, rather than a further sense of agitation.

HELENA RUTHERFURD ELY
(1858–1920)

She gardened in the grand manner and knew her gardening from the ground up. Her counsel on planting the small plot is authoritative and wise. Also, and this is highly unusual, she carefully considers costs. Admittedly, prices have increased since tulips were eighty cents for a hundred, but the principles are the same.

———

A Woman's Hardy Garden

How to Plant a Small Plot

I am frequently surprised to hear people say, "Oh, a flower garden is very nice, but such a trouble!" I have heard this expression several times from friends who employ a number of men and have large places with extensive lawns, shrubberies and vegetable gardens, but without flowers, except, perhaps, a few annuals growing among the vegetables.

Yet no one is indifferent to the beauty of a garden, or unobservant of the improvement which even a few flowers can make around the humblest cottage. Think of the pretty thatched cottages one sees everywhere in England and France, covered to the eaves with Roses and Clematis, and surrounded by flowers growing wherever they can find root in the tiny gardens. Yet all this is the result of only a half hour's daily care after the long day's work is done.

One should begin with a few plants—perhaps a dozen only—and the "trouble" will soon become a delight, unless one is devoid of all love for flowers.

Whenever I hear remarks on the "trouble" of a flower garden, I think of those peasant homes, and also of a little plot grown and cared for by a certain tenant farmer's wife I know. She has six children, and must cook and bake and clean for four men in addition; yet, some time every day, she finds a few minutes to tend her flowers. She has a border along the fence four by fifty feet, filled with perennials; a border across the front of her house with Phlox and Funkias,

Source: New York: The Macmillan Company, 1915.

and a couple of beds with Asters, Poppies, Balsams, Portulaca and Pinks. The perennials were given her, a few at a time. She separated the roots, saved the seeds to raise others, and has been able in this way to increase her borders. The seeds of the few annuals she buys do not cost more than a dollar a year. Thus, for a trifling expenditure and a short time every day, this woman makes her humble surroundings beautiful, while her soul finds an object upon which to expend its love of beauty, and her thoughts have a respite from the daily cares of life.

Many people have the mistaken idea that a flower garden, however small, is an expensive luxury, and are so convinced of this, that they never venture any attempt at gardening, and pass their lives knowing nothing of its pleasures.

Let us suppose some one is starting a suburban home in a simple way, and see how flowers can be had for many months at small cost. If one has a place in a town or village, the plot of ground not over fifty by two hundred feet, still the possibilities are great, and the owner can easily gather flowers for herself and her friends from April until mid-November. A house or cottage on such a piece of ground generally stands back from twenty to fifty feet, with a gravel or flagged walk running to the street. If the owner be a beginner in gardening and expects to do most of the work herself, let her commence with a few plants in a small space. As the plants thrive and become beautiful, the care of them will give an added pleasure to life, and, little by little, the beds and borders can be increased.

In beginning to plant a small plot, the most natural place first is a border, say two feet wide, on either side of the walk leading from the house to the street. Have these borders dug out and made properly. Then, if the owner wishes to see them continually abloom, bulbs must be planted, to give the early spring flowers. Tulips can be had for eighty cents a hundred, *Narcissus Poeticus* for sixty-five cents a hundred, and Yellow Daffodils for one dollar and twenty-five cents a hundred. Hyacinths are more expensive, and cost from four dollars a hundred up. If a hundred each of the Tulips, Narcissi, Hyacinths and Daffodils were planted they would make the borders lovely from early in April until late in May. The Daffodils will bloom first, then the Hyacinths, followed by the Narcissi, and the Tulips last, if care is taken to buy a late variety.

There should certainly be three or four Peonies in the borders,—pink, white, and dark red; good roots of these can be had for about thirty-five cents each. Once planted, they should not be disturbed for years; and, although the first season they may not yield more than two or three blossoms, in each succeeding year the flowers will increase in number. A friend told me, not long ago, that she had counted sixty blossoms upon each of several of her plants.

There should also be at least a dozen Columbines (Aquilegias) to bloom the end of May and the first of June. The roots of these can be bought for a dollar and a half a dozen, or they can be raised from seed; in the latter case, however, they would not bloom until the second year, being perennials.

No border can be complete without Delphiniums (Larkspur). Good-sized roots of the *Delphinium formosum,* lovely dark blue, are a dollar and twenty-five cents a dozen. *Formosum Cœlistina,* the light blue variety, is two dollars and a half a dozen. Then, of course, there must be other perennials,— Phlox, at least a dozen plants in the different colors, which will cost a dollar and a half.

A few Lilies will add greatly to the beauty of the borders. Tiger Lilies, which are only sixty cents a dozen; Auratums, which can be had from eighty-five cents a dozen up, according to the size of the bulbs; *Speciosum rubrum* from eighty-five cents a dozen up, and Candidums, or Madonna Lilies, a dollar and a half a dozen. German Iris, a dollar a dozen, and Japanese Iris, at a dollar and a quarter a dozen, should also have a place.

Excellent Gladioli can be bought for a dollar and fifty cents a hundred, and these will be most satisfactory if planted in the border about May fifteenth in groups of six to ten.

A dozen Chrysanthemums of the hardiest varieties to be obtained, and costing a dollar and a half a dozen, will, with the other plants mentioned, about fill two borders two feet wide by thirty long. It would also be well to sow the seeds of some Calendulas, Nasturtiums and Asters wherever there may be a vacant place. Or better, perhaps, sow the seeds in boxes in mid-April, and transplant to the border the early part of June. The first cost will be the only expense for these borders, except in the case of the Auratum Lilies, which will die out in about three years, and of the few flower seeds. The only care needed is to keep the borders free from weeds, to stir the soil every week, and to water after sunset in dry weather.

It will be seen, from the following list, that such borders can easily be made and planted at a cost of less than thirty dollars. This can be reduced by omitting the Hyacinths. . . .

Tulips	$0.80
Narcissi	.65
Daffodils	1.25
Hyacinths	4.00
Peonies	1.40
Columbines	1.50
Delphinium Formosum	1.25
Delphinium Cœlestina	2.50
Phlox	1.50

Tiger Lilies	.60
Auratum	.85
Lilium rubrum	.85
Lilium candidum	1.50
Japanese Iris	1.25
Iris Germanica	1.00
Chrysanthemums	1.50
Flower seeds	1.00
Three days' work, at $1.50 per day	4.50
Manure	1.50
TOTAL	$29.40

After a year or two, the owner of the cottage may want to increase the flower garden, and the next place to plant is close about the house. It is to be taken for granted that the house and piazzas have the proper gutters. This is necessary, of course, for the preservation of the house, and without gutters the drip from the eaves would be such that nothing could grow directly against the house.

The bed might be three feet wide and run across the front of the house on either side of the steps. The owner would probably wish to plant vines over the porch or piazza, in case it has not already been done. . . .

Should the house front the south, east or west, nearly everything can be grown; but should it face the north, nothing but Ferns and Rhododendrons would be successful on the front. Dahlias of the Cactus variety, in different colours, could be planted at the back of the bed on one side of the steps. Get good-sized roots, plant them two feet apart. They will grow against the house like a tall hedge. If planted the third week in April quite deep, say eight inches, they will begin to bloom about the sixth of July, and continue to be covered with flowers until killed by frost. In front of the Dahlias, plant white Phlox. In front of the Phlox sow a row of *Centaurea* or Cornflowers, the Emperor William variety. These should be sown early in April, will begin to bloom by June tenth, and, if they are not allowed to go to seed, will blossom all summer. Sow in front of the Cornflowers, at the same time, a row of white Candytuft, of the Empress variety. This also will bloom continuously if the flowers are cut as soon as they wither. On the other side of the steps, at the back of the bed, plant Rudbeckia (Golden Glow) two feet apart. The roots should be bought and planted, preferably in October, otherwise as soon as the frost is out of the ground in the spring, as they start very early. In front of the Rudbeckias plant Cannas—the Tarrytown, of most vivid scarlet hue, I have found the best and freest-flowering of all. The roots should be planted about May fifteenth.

On the edge of the bed, sow by April fifteenth a row of salmon-pink Zinnias, and when they are well up, thin out to six inches apart. They begin to blossom when very small, and will stand considerable frost. The expense of these beds will be trifling. Rudbeckias of the Golden Glow variety, one dollar a dozen; the Tarrytown Canna, two dollars and a half a dozen; Cactus Dahlias, two dollars a dozen; Phlox, one dollar and a half a dozen. The small quantity of flower seeds required will cost less than a dollar. A man can easily make the beds in three days. Therefore, the cost with manure will be less than fifteen dollars.

After a hard frost has killed the tops, the Dahlias, Cannas and Gladioli should be taken up, the tops cut off, the roots well dried, and then stored in a cellar that does not freeze. The Canna and Dahlia roots will have grown so large that they can be divided and it will be found that there are enough to plant, the following spring, nearly twice the space they occupied before.

It is impossible, if successful with the borders already planned, for the owner not to wish for more garden. She sees the neighbors' gardens with newly opened eyes; flowers and their treatment become an absorbing topic of conversation, and the exchange of plants a delightful transaction.

It will be seen that the next places to plant are along the boundary lines of the property. Even if one side only be laid out at a time, a large number of plants will be required. The owner will find great pleasure in raising as many of these herself as possible. To accomplish this, somewhere at the back of the place, a seed-bed should be made, and in April the seeds of perennials and annuals sown. The border must be made by September the twentieth and should be at least four feet wide. Either a hedge can be placed at the back of the border, or tall-growing flowering shrubs such as white and purple Lilacs (not the Persian), Mock Oranges (Syringa), Deutzia and Roses of Sharon (Althea). These shrubs will grow about equally high, yield an abundance of flowers, the Altheas in August, the others in May or June, and in four or five years will form a complete screen from the neighboring grounds.

In front of the shrubs perennials can be planted, taller ones at the back, lower-growing ones in front, and annuals along the edge. Such a border, if from fifty to one hundred feet in length, will be a garden by itself. The plants will do best if closely set, and every vacant space filled in June with annuals. Weeds then have little chance to grow, and a short time every day will keep such a border in order. The border can be of any width from four to twelve feet, but when more than four feet, the front edge should be made with irregular curves to avoid a stiff appearance.

Shrubs should be set out not later than October tenth, and, as they or the hedge would be at the back of the bed, the planting of them will not interfere with the perennials that have already been transplanted from the seed-bed. Hedges are so much more beautiful than any fence that ever was built that, in towns or villages where cattle are not allowed to run at large, hedges should, wherever possible, be used in place of fences.

To prepare the ground for a hedge, make a trench eighteen inches deep, put a good layer of well-rotted manure in the bottom and fill up with earth. When the hedge is planted, give it a good top-dressing of manure, and continue this top-dressing, with a little bone-meal sown on the surface of the ground, every spring.

The best and hardiest evergreen hedge is of Hemlock Spruce. Plants of this can be bought for fifteen dollars a hundred, and should be set eighteen inches apart.

The Privet is a favorite hedge in this country. It keeps green until December, and leafs out early in the spring. It is hardy and of rapid growth. Good plants are six dollars a hundred, and should be planted a foot apart. Catalogues say that if planted in rich soil one foot apart, a hedge five feet high can be grown in three seasons. Common Privet is more hardy than California Privet. *Hydrangea paniculata grandiflora* makes a beautiful low-growing hedge; good plants can be bought for six dollars a hundred. *Berberis Thunbergii,* or barberry, makes a fine hedge, on account of its beautiful foliage and scarlet fruit. It is, however, slow-growing.

The owner of a small place should avoid the temptation to scatter flower beds about the lawn. Keep all the planting along the edges of the property and around the house, and leave the lawn unbroken by flower beds. The years when gardening consisted only of beds of Coleus, Geraniums, Verbenas and bedding plants have passed away, like the black walnut period of furniture. And even as the mahogany of our grandfathers is now brought forth from garrets and unused rooms, and antiquity shops and farm-houses are searched for the good old-time furniture, so we are learning to take the old gardens for our models, and the old-fashioned flowers to fill our borders.

The nurseryman of today has greatly improved the size and colour of the old varieties of perennials, so that they are far more beautiful than formerly, and offer a much greater choice. By skillful hybridization a hundred or more kinds of Phlox have been developed. In the same way, numerous varieties of Delphiniums, Iris, Peonies, Columbines, Canterbury Bells and Foxgloves have been produced. The old-fashioned annuals also appear in many new forms. In addition to the pink and white "Painted Lady," the pure white and dark purple Sweet Peas of our mothers' time, we may now cultivate some eighty varieties of this delicate flower. Thus the garden of hardy perennials, annuals and bulbs will give us a continual sequence of flowers in every form and color from April until November, if properly made and tended.

RUTH BRAMLEY DEAN
(1880–1932)

Ruth Dean had an excellent reputation as a landscape architect, which was why she was asked to write for The Livable House *series. In the garden of the livable house, appropriateness in all types of planting design is given equal importance to the furnishings within the house. Ruth Dean also implies correctness, as in inviting guests to a dinner party who will mix harmoniously. Thinking of the plants in one's garden as one might think of the guests at one's table was an idea promoted by the women's magazines of the '20s; harmony was seated to the right of the hostess, and the hostess herself represented "good taste" with correctness on the left.*

THE LIVABLE HOUSE

ITS GARDEN

General Planting

Under the head of "General Planting" come all those miscellaneous kinds of planting which cannot be included in that of the garden proper. Foundation planting, border planting, the planting along drives and walks, screen planting, specimen planting, and miscellaneous flower planting—all of these are worth discussing separately, because very often one of these kinds, or a combination of two of them, constitutes all of the gardening which is done about a place.

Foundation planting, or the planting about the base of buildings, should have for its purpose not—as the nursery catalogue would lead one to believe—masking the foundations, but making the house look as if it belonged in its surroundings. There is nothing about an honest foundation wall that needs concealing, and it is unnecessary and undesirable that the house should grow out of a solid bank of shrubbery in order to hide something which, as likely as not, the architect has been at some pains to make interesting. A judicious amount of planting here and there about the house—at the corners or in angles, with something tall to carry the green line up where there are no windows, and lower growing things where there are—will take the raw new look away from a house and tie it down adequately to the lawn's green carpet.

Being Volume 2 of *The Livable House* Series, edited by Aymar Embury II.
Source: New York: Moffat Yard and Company, 1917.

The first requirement for the right sort of foundation planting, and, for the matter of that, the last too, is appropriateness. All the other requirements, namely strength, permanence, and proper scale, are included in this one term.

Probably the most common of the inappropriate sorts of foundation planting is that which appears to consist of one each of all the different kinds of evergreens contained in the nurseryman's catalogue. Every suburb and real-estate development abounds in houses whose foundations are surrounded with a lot of little yellow and green and blue balls, cones, and pyramids, which present a bristling, unnatural look and contribute nothing of repose or dignity to the house. What could be less appropriate, less calculated to make the house look as if it belonged to its particular bit of country, than this collection of "specimen" evergreens? "Specimens" is the term which most truly describes them, and as such they should be placed in arboretums. An exclusively evergreen planting is always bad because the trees are too decided and definite in form; they need the more graceful, branching, deciduous things to tie them together.

The chief quality on which evergreens rely for their popularity—the quality which endears them to most people—is their evergreenness. And, indeed, their color in the winter landscape is very desirable, but other colors than green contribute cheer to winter's dullness—and shrubs with colored berries and branches may be combined with the evergreens into a much more pleasing and natural-looking planting than one of evergreens alone. This is true of rhododendrons as well as of conifers, for a house which rises up out of a heavy somber bank of broad-leaved evergreens fits as poorly into the landscape as one whose base is concealed by ranks of little conifers.

Some of the berried shrubs which add to the agreeable appearance of a foundation planting, as much by their grace-

ful habit of branching as by their colored fruits, are the barberries—Thunbergii and vulgaris; high bush cranberry
(viburnum opulus), which provides from its bright clusters
food for the birds all winter long; other members of the
viburnum family; dentatum or arrow-wood, plicatum,
tomentosum, and Carlesii, which has a wonderfully fragrant
flower; the honeysuckles, Indian currant, and snowberry;
ilex Sieboldii (a little known but very brilliant berried shrub);
and the red stemmed dogwoods. Of these, berberis vulgaris
[sic], all the viburnums, the honeysuckles, and dogwoods
grow to be big shrubs and ought therefore to be planted
where they will not interfere with windows. Another shrub
with an impossible name but with the unusual possession of
turquoise colored berries is Symplocos Crataegoides. Its berries ripen at the same time as those of the Tartarian honeysuckle, and the two shrubs make a brilliant combination. Most
of these shrubs have attractive flowers as well as berries, and
thus provide at the same time for the summer and winter
appearance of the base planting. A few shrubs interesting
chiefly for their summer dress do not come amiss in any
group near the house, and some of them look especially well
with the dark foliage of evergreens: lilacs, white and purple;
deutzia, Pride of Rochester, pink weigelia, and spirea Van
Houttei are all good stand-bys which improve by their presence any planting of evergreens.

Another danger to be avoided in connection with evergreens near the house is the use of forest trees. In most cases,
either eagerness for a quick effect or ignorance of the real
character of the trees is responsible for their presence close
to the house. But whatever the cause, it is not an uncommon
sight to see the windows of houses five years or so old being
overgrown by hemlocks, white pines, spruces, and firs. These
are all big timber trees, and for this reason are extremely
inappropriate planted against a house wall. They belong out

where they have room to stretch and grow into the dignified trees Nature meant them to be.

Some of the smaller, less-spreading trees, such as cedars, arbor vitæ, and retinosporas, may be used against the house if they are planted where they will not come in the way of windows. At either side of an arch on the W. E. Seeley house at Bridgeport, cedars as well placed where they emphasize the entrance and will not grow out of bounds.

Quite at the opposite end of the scale from forest trees are flowers as a foundation planting, and for a correspondingly opposite reason they are inappropriate. I refer, as in the case of evergreens, to flowers used alone. Some of the stronger growing sorts, planted in connection with shrubs or vines, as Miss Coffin has used lilies and peonies along the piazza of the Edgar house, are both pleasing and appropriate; but the border of pinks and pansies or cannas and scarlet sage which very often forms the sole decoration around the base of a big house is too obvious a violation of the requirements of good foundation planting not to be censured.

Flowers alone lack strength and that feeling of permanence which good base planting should have, and, moreover, they are out of scale with the size of the house. They need shrubs or vines as a background to make them count as a mass rather than as individuals, and to leave something growing in their stead when they die down at the end of the season.

By the term border planting—the second of the miscellaneous sorts under the head of general planting—I mean combinations of shrubs, or shrubs and trees, such as one finds planted along a fence, substituted for a fence at the edge of a piece of property, around a garden, or at the end of the lawn. These borders divide themselves into two classes: naturalistic or woodland borders, and *gardenesque* or suburban.

They are two very different types, and a sharp line should be drawn between them, because, in practice, distinguishing the two makes all the difference between a commonplace garden and one with a really individual quality; or, in bigger landscape work, the contrast between a scheme grandly conceived and one which is petty in spirit.

The first sort of planting is made up of native trees and shrubs—those which grow naturally along meadow hedgerows or in woodland borders; this kind of border should be used away from the house and the cultivated garden, in places where a transition is to be effected between the wild and the cultivated, or where the spirit of native things is to be introduced or preserved. This bigger, freer sort of planting should be founded on the particular kind of landscape in which it occurs, and should follow Nature as closely as possible. A lowland border would not be composed of the same trees and shrubs as would an upland border, nor would either of these plantings be the same in Illinois and Massachusetts. Any naturalistic planting should express the character of the land where the border is being planted, so as to bring out the individuality of different parts of the country. Discard the bad characteristics of your especial piece of property, pick out its good features, and emphasize them, if you wish your garden different from your neighbor's, with a quality of its own.

If you have a stream on your place plant the borders near it with those shrubs and trees with grow in the neighborhood of water: alder, red-stemmed dogwood, the lacy, yellow-flowered spice bush, willows, birches (black and white), elderberry with its white panicles of fragrant flowers (which turn into berries that make the most delicious pie in the world), arrow-wood which also has white flowers—deceiving white flowers, for they tempt one into smelling them and then offer a vile reward; button bush, with its shining leaves and white balls—and an indefinite list of other friendly things, which like low places better than high.

And then if your border goes up hill, plant in it the shrubs which do not mind burning in the sun of a long hot July afternoon—sumach, wild roses, hawthorn, crabapple, sassafras, bayberry, red bud, and witch hazel. But above all things, in planting such a border as this, keep out the petty *gardenesque* feeling—one weigelia will ruin the character of a whole group of field plants; save the nursery shrubs for the flower garden and the planting near the house.

The converse of this warning is not true—any number of native shrubs and trees can be introduced into a border of lilacs and spireas and altheas, without hurting it in the least; but one shrub of this tamed company is enough to dispel the illusion of an entire naturalistic planting. The same strict rule is observable in connection with evergreens; cedars, white pines, Douglas spruce, and other native evergreens take their places very properly in woodland plantings, but retinosporas, cryptomerias, golden arbor vitæ, smack of the nursery—and destroy utterly the free spirit of the woods and fields.

Some landscape architects never get away from the suburban type of planting. Their *materia medica*, so to speak, consists of the contents of the nursery catalogues, and they treat a big park just as they would a little garden plot, using over and over again barberry, snowberry, forsythia, mock orange, and spireas, with perhaps a few native shrubs mixed in, out of deference to a dim idea that parks should be planted a little differently from small places. But the big conception that country is only to be introduced into city by means of fidelity to country planting, or that the spirit of existing country, its own particular charm, is to be preserved only by adherence to the example it sets, quite escapes them. A big meadow will never have the feel of a real meadow, will never be anything but an enlarged lawn, unless it be fringed with true meadow planting; the petty suburban feeling creeps in by way of privet and weigelia and deutzia—and the spirit of dogwood and hawthorn (the native kinds, not foreign introduced sorts), hazel nut, and sumach is gone.

I do not mean to be decrying the obvious merits of our faithful flowering shrubs; they are very useful and very beautiful, but I should like to make it clear that they are essentially of the house garden—that they have a tame cat feeling which belongs near the house, and that they should be left behind with the house when it is the spirit of woods and fields one is trying to recall in planting. These principles are true of the elements of planting along drives and walks according as the groups of shrubs and trees are near the house or remote from it.

The form which the planting should take depends upon the form of the drive or walk.

The avenue type of planting, that is straight rows of things, should be confined to walks or drives which are straight; irregular lines demand irregular planting—both as to height and breadth—and a drive which twists and curves should not be bordered by straight ranks of trees and bushes of even height.

It is probably unnecessary to say that no drive or walk should curve without appearing to curve for a reason, and if it curves just for the sake of curving an excuse has to be supplied. Under some circumstances it so happens that it is undesirable to fill up all the bends of a road with bushes; they are apt to give a shut-in feeling to the drive which at certain points is unpleasant. A tree or a clump of trees in such a position furnishes the needed excuse for a turn and at the same times does not produce the confining effect of a solid mass of bushes.

The off side, so to speak, of a curve is less important as to planting. The group of bushes or trees, if any are used on this side of the drive, should consist of kinds similar to those on the opposite side, and may be carried back away from the drive . . . , with low growing stuff in front to emphasize the bay, and higher growing things behind. Correspondingly, the point on the opposite side might be marked by high shrubs, although observance of the demands of automobilists who must be able to see along the entire length of a drive, is fast leveling off all border planting.

There is a purely sentimental reason for making the planting in a bend high, to which I, who do not mind driving slowly along a curving road, am inclined to cling, and that is the pleasure of not knowing what lies just ahead. Mystery always has its charm, and I would rather be surprised by coming out of a wood suddenly onto a green stretch of lawn than know all along that presently we shall be running at the edge of the green velvet strip, which I can see across the low bushes.

Screen planting, the fourth kind of general planting, may consist of irregular borders of shrubs and trees, or of hedges. The latter are usually regarded as the logical means of screening a service drive, or laundry yard, or unneighborly nuisance. They are the most obvious form of screen, the form most often used, and in some ways the least effective, for their purpose is generally as apparent as that of a trellis or wall would be. Like these they need planting outside to tie them into the general landscape.

Any kind of clipped hedge is, of course, slower in attaining height than plants which are allowed to grow unchecked by the pruning shears. It follows that a free-growing border will screen faster and more effectively than a hedge. But the most valid reason for giving any irregular planting preference is that it can be made a part of the landscape. When a hedge is used either for a screen or as the boundary of a garden it should have something in the way of transition planting outside it—a few groups of shrubs and trees to break the definite form and regular line of the hedge, and to "ease" it into its surroundings.

Of the deciduous hedges, probably privet is the most common and the most useful. It is obligingly adaptable, grows quickly, and has a dignified appearance. Barberry makes a somewhat smaller hedge, never growing over four or five feet high, and is more spreading in character. Some effort has been made to introduce hornbeam and beech as hedges. These are both good, dignified hedges, and along with our native hawthorns could be utilized delightfully around gardens; but their slow growth and greater cost too often combine to make the weedier privet a favorite.

Among evergreens, more fame attaches to the name of box than to any other kind of hedge. It is truly the aristocrat among hedges, and an old specimen commands respect and veneration from a hurrying generation, which appreciates to the full its meager inheritance but fails to provide for its children any more generously.

It is only human to want immediate returns on an investment, to plant for an early effect, to be impatient of waiting for results; and yet a garden should be planned with some eye to permanence as well, and the poplars that go in because of their rapid growth should be tempered with timber trees to give dignity to the garden a decade hence, and a beech hedge started wherever possible to overawe the privet by and by, or one of hawthorn, which will cover its twisted old stems with white blossoms in the spring and red apples in the fall.

To return to evergreen hedges, both dwarf arbor vitæ and the yews (taxus brevifolia and brevifolia cuspidata) make a good low hedges; and hemlock, arbor vitæ, and cedar are all more or less dependable high hedges. Of these, arbor vitæ turns rusty in the winter and hemlock sometimes "kills back," but at the height of its glory hemlock probably comes nearest to possessing that dark, solid green appearance of English yew hedges, which is so much the envy of us in our drier climate.

Ilex—of somewhat doubtful hardihood in Northern winters—trims well into a hedge, and has no other fault than its great expense.

Perhaps a word as to the form to which hedges should be trimmed would not come amiss. If the hedge be appreciably wider at the top than it is at the bottom it holds the snow in winter, which is apt to break apart the bushes, and prevents both moisture from reaching the roots and a full amount of sunlight from coming to the lower portions of the hedge. For these reasons a hedge trimmed straight up and down or with a wider base than top, is better than one of a wedge shape.

The term "specimen planting" immediately conjures up pictures of a lawn spotted over with blue spruces and Japanese red maples—and weeping mulberries. This is the sort of planting which has attached unpleasant association to the term "specimen planting," and all but limited its use to such a meaning. But there are appropriate places for specimen trees and bushes of the right sort—although there is no place for exotic-looking specimens but the museum or arboretum.

The general rule of keeping centers of lawns and open spaces clear and confining the planting to borders, with the possible exception in the case of big spaces to a very limited number of judiciously planted groups, is familiar to every one in this day of the ubiquitous garden article. But too rigid an interpretation of the rule is apt to result in wall-like borders; these may be broken here and there, and points may be brought out or emphasized by the use of individual trees and bushes. Such points as these offer opportunities for planting the especially fine bush or tree, the good qualities of which one wishes to exhibit.

The corners of flower beds, doorways, and gates, avenues—such prominent places as these call for the picked or specimen plant. . . .

There are certain sorts of flower plantings which come under no general head, and are pleasures to the eye, others which are just messy and purposeless. Of the first, one of the most pleasing kinds is spring bulbs naturalized in grass. Nothing is lovelier than narcissus and Virginia cowslip blooming in stretches of white and blue—or the little grape hyacinth flashing its blue near the yellow dandelion which flowers at the same time—or masses of purple hyacinths and golden daffodils.

Other flowers, for the most part native ones, are good naturalized in bold groups, or planted in, here and there, with shrubbery. For the latter kind of planting, flowers which are woodland in character or strong growing flowers are best: foxgloves, columbines, echinops—the showy orange helenium, asters, boltonia, monkshood—are all more or less colorful in a border of shrubs, for they flower in sufficient masses to make themselves felt.

But most flowers should be collected into a flower garden, however small it may be, rather than be scattered about in promiscuous beds and borders. They count for more arranged together in this way because it is possible to get bigger stretches of color at once. The flowers can be cared for more easily and profitably, and the chances are they leave the rest of the place looking tidier and less cluttered. A wavy border of perennials following the outlines of a shrub border is rarely a success, for the flower borders are seldom wide enough to count, and they succeeded only in imparting a ragged look to the shrubs. A straight border against a hedge, if the place is not large enough for a garden, or a wide border along a walk, is more effective than the wavy ribbon of a curving border following the outlines of shrubs.

Of flowers about foundation walls I have spoken in the first part of this chapter. For garden walls, rules are less rigid; here the idea of permanence in planting is not so important, and although the appearance of the wall and the flower borders both benefit by vines and an occasional shrub planted against the wall, these are not the necessities demanded by a house wall. The planting at the base of the Hubbard pergola is a pleasing combination of vines, wall surface, and flowers.

The final test to which any of the kinds of planting listed at the beginning of the chapter must be put, is that of appropriateness. The object of each especial planting must be considered, the purpose for which it is planted, or the atmosphere it is designed to produce, and those shrubs, trees, and flowers used which will contribute to this effect. Types of planting are just as distinct as human beings, with personalities as different, and they must be arranged with the same care one expends in choosing guests at a dinner party, if the effect is to be harmonious and satisfying.

ELSA REHMANN
(b. 1886)

Elsa Rehmann seems, almost better than anyone else, to understand what it means to be a gardener. She speaks directly, as one gardener to another. I would so much like to make an August garden as described here—in fact it seems almost irresistible. She is not only knowledgeable about plants, but she strives for practicality and beauty with a balance that is unique. She writes with passion and authority.

GARDEN-MAKING

The Simplest Kind of Garden

The simplest kind of garden is a flower-bordered path. Its simplicity lies in the singleness of its purpose and in the directness of its composition. Despite the elemental character of its design, however, it can reach sublime perfection in proportion; despite its straightforward sincerity, it can be elaborated with exquisite detail; despite all its limitations, it can be wrought into a wonderful completeness.

Try to visualize a typical example. It seems so easy, doesn't it? Just a flower-bordered path, and yet you become ensnared straightway [sic] in the tangle of its infinite variety. There is a path, I remember, that wanders through a woodland, finding its delight in primroses and violas, in forget-me-nots and Anchusa myosotidiflora [sic], in columbines and mertensias. There is another path I know, carved in the slope of a hill where, beneath a wall overhung with a wealth of intermingled rose climbers and buddleias with soft summer bloom, there are narrow borders filled with polyantha roses. There is a third path beneath the sun-flecked tunnel of a long grape arbor where Japanese anemones find a welcome haunt. There is a path that climbs its wonderful way up and up, flight upon flight, between hemlocks and pines, with all sorts of tumbling plants along the edges. And, finally, there is a path in an orchard where fascinating medleys of spring flowers spread out beneath blossoming fruit-trees.

There are paths that find their greatest pleasure in di-

Source: Boston: Houghton Mifflin Company, 1926.

rectness. Straight as an arrow, they become impersonations of that familiar axiom, a line that is the shortest distance between two points. And then, there are paths that, molding themselves to contours and fitting themselves to circumstance, wind their ways graciously like languid streams. Some paths fit on level ground and others like to wind up a hillside. Some are brilliant and sunny, others like the deep shade and half shade of woodsy places. Some are so narrow that we find ourselves in constant peril of treading upon the flower edges, while others are so generously wide as to allow two people to stroll leisurely along with a dog by their side.

The width of the walk depends partly upon the material used, but mainly upon circumstance. Few realize, however, that the width of a path can determine not only the amount of physical comfort, but the degree of sensory pleasure there is in walking through a garden. A path of two or three feet is too narrow, in any case; a path of eight feet is commensurate with a big design; a path of five or even six feet is usually in proper proportion and comfortable.

The width of the borders, too, depends upon circumstance. I have found, however, that five-foot borders are usually too reserved and unmindful of flower habits. They may be very nice upon a plan, but in actuality they not only put strict limitations upon the flower selection, but give the garden a cramped and stingy look. I never feel free to use any tall or free-spreading flowers in them, no hollyhocks or heleniums, no dahlias or perennial asters, for instance. Eight- or ten-foot borders are much happier in looks, are usually sufficient and possible from a working point of view. I have found that, even in a rather small garden, ten-foot borders accommodate themselves quite nicely. They may look too wide in plan, but even a rough cross-section will give you the effect that flower heights and background shrubs and hedges have upon the width of the garden. These are all niceties in proportion which must be sensitively felt to be really appreciated.

Sometimes the borders must be self-contained and the flowers carefully distributed for height and color; again, these path gardens may give way to all sorts of vagaries. The borders may be now wide, now narrow; the flowers now high, now low; the bloom now abundant, now meager; the color now brilliant and boisterous, now faint and fairy-like. I like a little cozy path where you can tuck all those darling little things that are not effective in a real garden. There is often a chance for such a path in a vacant corner. All the little edging plants are especially welcome there, for each little variety can be noticed, so close at one's feet it is. I want violas there in all their fascinating variety, and for very contrast with them the saxifrages. I want creeping veronicas and all the dainty kinds of dianthus. I want tunicas and nierembergias. I like these plants in irregular masses and delightfully intermingled and planted so near the edge of the border that they spread over the path with freedom. I like these paths to be of broken paving, for such plants spoil the edges of grass paths in their very exuberance and look forlorn when they come in contact with gravel. I would rather have these wondrously free edgings with all their varied bloom and varied habit than even boxwood edgings for all their beauty, and I would forsake the most wonderful of great gardens for one of these little cozy paths.

There are paths that can take upon themselves the very character of their surroundings. There are paths bordered with boxwood and enclosed with fine walls or evergreen hedges that fit rich houses and luxuriant settings. There are paths bordered with lilacs, altogether old-fashioned, rugged paths through fields with wild roses and meadow-sweets, paths between trained espalier fruit in vegetable gardens, paths tunneled beneath clipped hornbeams or bounded by trained lindens in a quaint and Old-World spirit.

Then, there are paths that will interpret the character of their sites. I remember a fine old house sheltered by great trees. From the central doorway you look down a long flower-bordered path. The grass walk is seven, perhaps eight feet wide; the borders are ten or twelve at least. Path and borders together are as wide as the house itself. This gives the garden a generous feeling quite beyond its actual dimensions. There is, too, a perfect relationship between the length of the path and the height of the trees, between the undulating flower masses and the width of the tree branches.

Then, there are paths that absorb the very character of the natural scene about them. I know a path that winds down from the house through flower borders to a boat-house standing on one of the little inlets of the Sound. It has a great S-shaped curve like the streams we see winding lazily through flat meadow-lands. In the spring goldentuft spreads its flat bloom over the pavement and the grayish foliage of Nepeta mussini [sic] is overspread with a haze of filmy blossoms. Saxifrages are showing their pink spires above great leaf rosettes, and thyme and sedums intermingle the varying grays of their foliage along the way. Everything is flat and matlike as if to interpret the very mood of the level meadow-land all around. Then, later on, the borders become more rugged with bolder and coarser plants. Some are those we can find in the fields, butterfly weeds and evening primroses, tansies and goldenrods and the cow-parsnip that we have seen standing out boldly above the wet lands above sluggish streams. Then, there are such decorative plants as plumepoppies, and such rugged plants as globethistles that have a picturesque growth reminiscent of wind-swept dunes. In all these plants, in their rugged habits and in their bold outlines, we find the spirit of the wild meadow-land in summer.

There are paths that delight in exhibiting a single flower, iris or peony, foxglove or aster, dahlia or chrysanthemum. The uniformity of kind is offset by manifold differences in color and by the individualities of diverse varieties. In this type of garden, the flower must be of sufficient interest to be very telling in bloom and effective in habit. It must be so enchanting for the few weeks that it flowers, as to make up for the lack of bloom for the rest of the season. This type of path is often a specialist's garden and sometimes it is a delightful element in a vegetable garden. Usually it requires ample dimensions for its charm, and yet I have seen such single effects carried to great perfection in little gardens. I remember one in which there was a succession of hyacinths, Canterbury bells, and chrysanthemums, each carried out in a graded sequence of color that was quite enchanting.

Paths seem to divide themselves according to their intent. There are paths that, as 'a way in,' become introductory phases to larger garden units. Sometimes these paths are very dignified with accents of magnolias, holly, yews, or boxwood; sometimes even little paths are worth-while a bit of careful study, like one not more than fifteen feet long leading from porch to garden between closely planted spiræas and snowberries, where in the narrow space left for flowers there are white pinks and sweet alyssum, lavender verbenas and heliotrope, poet's narcissus and white daffodils. Most paths are just 'a way through' from one part of the grounds to another, where the character of the planting has a transitional aspect and where gates or gateways, rose arches or arbors, sometimes mark beginning and end. Some paths, however, become real little flower gardens. This type is, perhaps, more difficult to plan than either of the other two, for there are niceties in the relationship of its parts that can be overlooked in 'a way through' and there are subtleties in its details that can be omitted in 'a way in.'

This kind of a garden is based upon the simplest of compositions. It has one axis and one focal point. This focal point is of great importance. It can give the garden its reason and emphasize its character. It can be the most precious statue or the simplest seat; it can be the most elaborate teahouse or the simplest arbor; brick wall, marble coping, and bronze statue can be combined into the richest of terminal features or a simple wall fountain sunk beneath a dry-laid wall overspread with rock-plant bloom may be quite adequate if the character of the garden permits. A sympathetic accord between the important elements of a garden is of great importance in determining its character. Widening the path in front of this terminal feature gives it proper emphasis; putting it in a niche or apse-like place gives it impressiveness; backgrounds of tall trees give it setting and frame.

There is need, too, to enclose the garden, and for this there are walls and lattices, clipped hedges and free-growing flowering ones in the greatest variety to fit every requirement.

Such simple compositions often require variation. The charm of one garden I know is due to the contrast that exists between the shady and the sunny parts of the path. At first, in the shade, it is all a quiet green, for from the porch steps we enter an arbored way. Actinidia, trumpetvine, and grape cover the rustic beams, while funkias and ferns cover the ground below. Then, out in the sunlight, we come upon borders with gay flowers and enclosing lattices covered with climbing roses. There is another path where the first third of its length is given over to rose beds that are edged with heliotrope and forms an introduction to the flowers that border the rest of the way. The hedges that enclose the path also divide one part from the other. There is still another part where a rose garden interrupts its length, and a fourth garden where a round pool divides the path in two.

These path gardens have all the problems of other gardens in the opportunities that they offer for well-studied succession of bloom, flower distribution, and color effectiveness. In one garden I know, a medley of intermingled color is full of interest; in another, a more restrained scheme of blue and yellow flowers in ample variety of shade and tone is effective. In a third, each color is used in a separate section by itself. In still another, the color is arranged in a kind of sequence. This is a very interesting experiment. The sequence starts with pink flowers. The first bloom is of pyrethrums and Canterbury bells and lupines. Then, in midsummer there are hollyhocks, and in the autumn closely planted gladioli rise up amid bushy snapdragons and mingled with them are occasional anemones and pink lilies. Quite unexpectedly, we find in this pink scheme a few yellow touches, creamy irises, pale *Digitalis ambigua,* soft yellow meadow-rues, and golden eremurus. They seem but accidental, a glint, a spot, a line of yellow harmony. Beyond these, the flowers are white, blue, yellow, lilac, and red. First, there are white columbines, white phloxes, white hollyhocks, white anemones, and white stocks; then there are flowers like Iris Madame Chereau that are part white, part blue, and flowers like *Delphinium cœlestinum* and *Salvia farinacea* where the blue coloring seems laid thinly over white, until we reach the deeper blues of columbines and larkspurs.

Then yellow flowers predominate. In late May, for instance, there is a group of yellow day lilies with erect yellow irises rising behind and yellow columbines near by. I think I like the borders best in the autumn when the red flowers are at their best. Think of brick-red verbenas and tritomas and fiery-red dahlias together at the end of one border and in the opposite border deep-red dahlias standing beside violet New England asters, the one a contrast of complementary colors becoming soft through the perfect modulation of its tones, the other an exultant concord.

It may seem at first glance, perhaps, that the borders at either side of this path are arranged rather arbitrarily into a color programme. There is nothing fixed or conventional about it, however, for while each color is used in distinct masses, it is then partly mingled with the next, so that the colors are never seen as isolated groups, but as blended masses. Even the quantity of the color is never the same: now it is a bold mass, again a mere suggestion, so that its effect in connection with other colors is always new. The flowers, too, are planted with such freedom and naturalness that the effects seem entirely unstudied, and yet it is this very color progression that underlies the charm of each and every effect.

These little path gardens allow, too, for many charming little changes from year to year as one's desires form and multiply. A little garden I know finds a new color scheme in Darwin tulips each spring and each summer a different arrangement of annuals. One summer there were white, blue, and yellow flowers in the borders. The next year had much the same effects with an added touch of maroon in snapdragons and cherry color in dahlias. The next year the border became much brighter and livelier. Tagetes and buff snapdragons and orange calendulas were mingled with ageratum along the edges of the path, masses of blue stock-flowered larkspurs and blue salvia were enlivened by orange zinnias and *Gladiolus primulinus* and the background was filled with orange dahlias. That is the real joy of a garden; every year promises a new venture, leading you from the simplest of experiences into the color wealth of flowers.

LOUISE BEEBE WILDER
(1878–1938)

She is such a pleasure to read, and she writes with such authoritative dignity that one imagines every single word to be true! Pleasures and Problems of a Rock Garden *was first published in 1928 and it quickly became a classic. Now, more than sixty years later, it is still unsurpassed for sheer engaging brilliance. Louise Beebe Wilder's notes on construction are succinct and very valuable.*

PLEASURES AND PROBLEMS
OF A ROCK GARDEN

Brief Hints on Construction

It is not possible to prescribe exact directions for the building of a rock garden. Each situation will require a different treatment, and every builder will cherish some idea of the effect he wishes to bring about. Often the conformation of the ground chosen for the rock garden settles the matter of what type is to be built—a high slope, a valley, a glen, each presupposing a definite type of construction. Again the kind and size of the stones at our command determine or restrict to a great degree what we are able to accomplish.

If the available situation happens to be a slope with natural outcroppings of rock nothing could be more fortunate provided the exposure is a genial one. In this case the work is half done and at a minimum of expense. On the other hand, if the only space to be had is perfectly level, then all the wit, the taste, the vision of the builder must be brought into play to make the finished garden appear like a stretch of naturally rugged landscape, harmonious and coherent in all its parts, and of a piece with its surroundings. Not at all is this situation to be regarded as hopeless, however, nor even exceptionally difficult; but it will take more labour and more material, and the builder must be able clearly to visualize the form he wishes his miniature landscape to take and to work patiently toward it. He will be doing all the work unassisted by nature, but he may,

Source: Garden City, N.Y.: Doubleday, Doran & Company, Inc., 1928.

nevertheless, contrive a beautiful rock garden wherein homes for the choicest rock plants may be found. The greatest difficulty, perhaps, will be to reconcile it to its surroundings, so that it will not appear alien and out of place. But as Mr. Farrer* wrote, if you want a beautiful rockery as well as beautiful plants, you must work it out for yourself. And this is true. For the rest, here are a few general principles that will help make the world of the garden safe for our Lilliputian democracy.

THE SITUATION

Of course, the ideal situation does not fall to the lot of many of us. Indeed, I am not quite sure what the ideal situation would be; it depends, it seems to me, upon what one wants to do. But for growing a wide variety of sun-loving rock plants and alpines, and a lesser number of shade lovers—and this is the aim of most rock gardeners—I would choose a piece of sloping ground (not too steep) quite out in the open, away from buildings, hedges, fences, all formal adjuncts and artificial construction, and well out from under overhanging branches, where a free circulation of air is assured and plenty of sunshine. You can build in northern exposures and shaded hollows for such plants as crave them, but it is not possible to contrive sunshine, and this is the desire of the heart of most alpines.

That the fall of the rock garden should be from north to south is considered very desirable[,] this general slope providing many planting sites having easterly and westerly exposures. A fall from south to north is much less available from the point of view of growing alpines; even a slight

* Farrer, Reginald (1880–1920). Plant collector and author, known especially for his works on rock gardening.—Ed.

slope to the north creates a cold exposure, and while this is satisfactory to a number of plants, it is not for the great majority.

North of the rock garden, it is a wise provision to mass evergreens and early-flowering shrubs and small trees as a protection from the bitter winds of winter, and if there are a few tall trees away to the east, the frozen leaves and blossoms of the early spring will be saved the kiss of the morning sun which is so often fatal to them. Care should be observed that the setting of trees and shrubs usually necessary to tie the rock garden into the surrounding landscape should not be of a character or proximity to shut off light and air from the plants. For the most part, the surrounding shrubs and trees should be dwarf of stature with a few taller subjects for accent. Evergreen and deciduous things should be equally resorted to, but simple groupings of a few kinds are more effective than conglomerate assemblages. A few early-flowering deciduous shrubs in the neighourhood of the rock garden add greatly to the modest display made by the early rock plants. A selection might be, if the garden is of fair size, the spring Witch-hazels, *Hamamelis mollis* and *H. japonica*, *Daphne mezereum*, *Chaenomales* [sic] (*Cydonia*) *japonica* or Japanese Quince in several lovely colours, Spice Bush, *Cornus Mas*, *Magnolia stellata*, Corylopsis of several kinds, Japanese Cherries, Peaches, and Crabapples.

It has already been pointed out that a piece of sloping ground obviates much labour and makes easily possible a delightful type of rock garden. But, failing this, almost any site may be contrived into an effective bit of landscape and a happy home for a great variety of plants. A possible situation often overlooked is a grassy bank, in most instances difficult to keep tidy and usually ragged in appearance. By removing the sod and cleaning the place thoroughly of grass roots and digging in a little good earth and sand, then planting the stones so that each lies a little farther back than the other, leaving between them crevices and niches wherein all sorts of little tufts and bulbs and tiny shrubs may be inserted, a most gay and interesting rock garden may be materialized where before was a dull expanse of no interest whatever.

Assuming that the site chosen for the rock garden lies on the level or on a gentle slope, the first thing to do is to mark off the area that is to be brought under treatment. Whatever its size, let the outline be broadly irregular, not fussily broken up or evenly scalloped. Stakes may be used to define the boundaries, or a small trench dug to mark the outline more clearly. When the size and shape have been determined, the earth should be dug out to a depth of at least a foot—more if the situation is low and apt to be damp. This is to insure drainage, but, of course, if the slope is steep, almost no artificial drainage will be required. Into the excavation should go broken stones, clinkers, pieces of rock, anything that will insure the ready draining away of superfluous moisture which is so unwholesome for many rock plants. On top of the drainage material a layer of sods, grass side down, should be placed, to prevent the soil from percolating through the loose material. Over the sods, several inches of coarse soil may be thrown, and the foundation is then ready.

THE STONES

The chief end of a rock garden, it should be understood, is not the stones. Their mission is simply to provide safe and comfortable quarters for a wide variety of plants. The aim is not a garden of rocks, as would sometimes seem to be the case, but a great number of delightful plants flourishing in a rocky situation. But we should, nevertheless, make the most of our stones, considering them carefully when they are assembled, and setting aside the best pieces, those that are fine in shape and nicely weathered, for the most prominent positions. The beauty of the rock garden is largely dependent upon the beauty and suitableness of the stones. Often, of course, we must use just what comes to hand or what is the most easily to be got at, but even among these there will be a choice, and it pays to make it with care. The poorer pieces may be buried as the construction rises and the finest kept for showing above ground.

It is preferable, where possible, to make use of one type of stone throughout the construction; this is the first step toward making it a harmonious whole. Sandstone or limestone are the best types to use, both from the point of view of the comfort and health of the plants and of the appearance of the rock garden. Freshly quarried stone or cut stone is rather too new and raw to create a happy effect, but, on the other hand, the square or rectangular forms often taken by such stones make building very easy, and very soon the small creepers and mantling shrubs, assisted by the kindly finger of time, blur the raw surfaces, and the effect is not so bad. The poorest to use are rounded field stones. With these it is impossible to make a stable construction; they are apt to turn over if stepped on, frost easily dislodges them, and it is impossible to pack earth about them in such a way that it will not presently come sifting out. Stones that are more or less absorbent are enjoyed by the plants, their searching roots clinging about them and finding moisture in the crevices. Very soft stone is unsatisfactory for the reason that it is apt to disintegrate under heavy frosts, undermining our constructing and often bringing our careful work to ruin. Tufa* is a calcareous water deposit "rock," in the fissures and indentations of which many small plants find most felicitous homes.

---

* Tufa is a calcareous deposit of rather porous character precipitated from solution by lime-charged waters, and not to be confused with the volcanic "tuff."

It is too spectacular and artificial in effect to use freely, but pieces may be incorporated in the rock work and used to accommodate certain small Saxifrages, tiny Pinks, and the like. Granite is hard and unsympathetic, but if you are under the necessity of making use of just what is at hand, this or any other stone can be made to do.

THE CONSTRUCTION

It is of the first importance before beginning to build to have all the material on the spot. This greatly facilitates building. A few very large rocks add immensely to the dignity and nobility of the scene, so an effort should be made to secure a few. These should not be placed low down in the construction, as is often done, but should lie along the heights as they would in nature. The massive outcroppings of rock appear naturally at the summit while smaller stones and broken stuff are found at the bottom. A reversal of this natural arrangement creates a weak and unconvincing effect.

From the first, one should set out to create beauty quite apart from the plants. "When the compilation is finished," wrote Mr. Farrer, "it ought to look established, harmonious and of a piece, long before a single tuft has been put in place." This is the ideal to work toward. Begin by scrutinizing the staked area attentively, trying the while to realize its possibilities. Then endeavour to form a mental picture of a natural scene that might be materialized within its boundaries—a little range of hills, irregular in outline, but never spectacular, or if the rock garden is to be very small, a single mountain, broad and irregular and sloping gently from the summit, not after the manner of a successful pudding, but thrusting out massively and unevenly, forming bays and gorges as a proper mountain would.

When the picture is clear in the mind, the main paths should be laid out. These should be narrow and pleasantly meandering and designed to reach all parts of the construction. Flat, irregularly shaped stones make the best paths, but simple earth paths are quite in keeping. Bluestone, gravel, or turf appear too artificial to fit into the picture. To increase the natural appearance of the construction, it is effective to build out a rocky shoulder or place a large stone where the paths make a turn to create the illusion that the divergence was necessary. When the compilation is completed, stepping stones may be placed here and there over the hills to facilitate getting about.

To start the construction, the earth from the excavation may be mixed with broken stone, large and small, and piled in along the paths to form the foundation of our little hills, or whatever form the construction is to take, the paths taking their places in the scheme as valleys winding between the hills. Then begin building at the bottom, piling up the earth and stones as nearly as possible in the likeness of the picture conceived, covering some stone entirely to strengthen the construction, allowing others to thrust out of the earth to form massive abrupt shoulders, ledges, terraces, sheer declivities, in the clefts of which many a small plant will delight to grow. Each stone should appear as much as possible as if it belonged to some great underlying ledge of rock. "See that your rock work is not disjointed in effect, but so ordered that each rock looks as if it belonged to the next, and had been its bedfellow since the foundations of the hills were made." To this end, here are a few unalterable laws to be followed:

Do not cast stones haphazard over a mound of earth; each must be firmly set with method and intention.

To insure permanent stability, each stone should be buried at least a third in the earth.

Each stone should lie upon its broadest base, as it would

in nature; never should it be stood on end. The spike rock garden had quite a vogue at one time, but it is a vulgar travesty upon nature and a most unlikely home for plants.

Each stone should slope back toward the bank behind it in order that moisture may be directed toward the roots of the plants instead of away from them.

The construction should not overhang at any point, as plants growing at the base would be cut off from the rainfall.

See that the earth is thoroughly rammed about every stone. This is all-important, for air pockets are death traps for prowling roots, and it is impossible to remedy this serious defect when once the construction is finished.

If the rock used is stratified, it will add immensely to the realistic beauty and reposefulness of the garden if the lines of stratification are matched.

To increase the apparent difference in height between hill and valley, we may resort to planting. For the most part, plant high on the heights; a small evergreen or little deciduous shrub, or some hardy plant whose stems aspire, such as Iceland Poppies, Columbines, the medium-sized Pentstemons, will greatly aid illusion. A little tree used in such a situation should be of spreading form, crooked, and as if contorted by the fury of many storms in an exposed position. Bushy, spreading plants are most effective near the base with the higher regions reserved for the smaller, choicer things. Thus, in nature, we leave behind the coarser growths as we climb the mountain, finding the smaller treasures higher up.

Early autumn is a good time to build a rock garden, and it should be allowed to stand over the winter unplanted in order that it may have a chance to settle and mould itself into its ultimate form. The canny builder chooses the site of his rock garden where it may be added to, for one of the first things he will realize when it is completed is that it is far too small.

MARJORIE SEWELL CAUTLEY
(1892–1954)

*This book was extremely well received by such diverse critics
as Lewis Mumford and Katherine T. Cary of the Garden
Club of America. Cary thought the "whole book is perfectly
wonderful—it is an outstanding piece of work and nothing
that I know of in the market is one-tenth as good. . . ." She
also acknowledged the clarity of thought and presentation in
the following excerpt, writing that "the color chapter
should sell the book alone."*

GARDEN DESIGN
THE PRINCIPLES OF ABSTRACT
DESIGN AS APPLIED TO
LANDSCAPE COMPOSITION

Color

"For those who intend to use color in creative work, a certain amount of theory is indispensable, as it simplifies the subject and opens up a few definite lines of research."
DOW

"Color systems and methods of describing and classifying colors date back hundreds of years. Chevreul, the pioneer in this field, although he did excellent work, did not influence the practical users of color because his color classification was based arbitrarily on the irregularities of dye and pigment mixture, which are very difficult to retain in one's memory. Only a method of color notation that is simple to understand and easy to remember can adequately fill the practical needs of present day color users.

"The great scientist, Helmholtz, gave considerable thought to this question. He stated that color possesses three simple attributes or dimensions, which are determined directly by the eye, and which

Source: New York: Dodd, Mead & Company, 1935.

have no direct relation to dye or pigment mixtures. As he did not have the opportunity to illustrate just how these three dimensions were to be visualized, however, nor what standards should be set up for developing a general color language, his work remained for a time buried in the archives of science.

"In the late [eighteen-] nineties, it occurred to an instructor of art, Mr. Albert M. Munsell, to utilize the possibilities opened up by Helmholtz in practical color study. Mr. Munsell decided that the best way to bring about a popular understanding of this subject was to illustrate the three dimensions of color graphically on a color sphere. He therefore planned a series of color charts presenting carefully standardized scales of *Hue, Value,* and *Chroma.*

"*Hue* is the name of a color. It is the property by which any color of the spectrum is distinguished from the other colors.

"Passing a ray of sunlight through a prism breaks the light up into a band of its component colors—the spectrum."

(Spectrum or rainbow colors visible to the eye are *Red-Yellow-Green-Blue-Violet.* Invisible light rays in long wave lengths are called infra-red, while invisible light rays in short wave lengths are called ultra-violet.)

"*Value* is the lightness or darkness of a color. For instance, yellow is usually a light color, nearer to white than to black. Purple-blue is usually a dark color, nearer to black. . . . By comparing any color with the different greys of the scale it is easy to distinguish the value of that color.

"*Chroma* is the strength or weakness of a color. It is the property which governs the intensity or purity of a color." Example—Bright Blue or Dull Blue.

(The standard or normal value of a color is that value at which the color reaches its maximum intensity. Different colors reach maximum intensities at different values.)

"To notate any color according to the Munsell Theory, it is only necessary (1) to choose its *Hue* in the sequence of colors around the Color Sphere; (2) to indicate its *Value* according to the *Neutral* scale axis of the Sphere; and (3) its *Chroma* according to the Chroma Scales of color strength. The *Munsell Book of Color* provides scientifically accurate color charts for the purpose."*

Any color, whether light or dark, bright or dull, can be defined exactly according to the Munsell System of Color Notation, by using letters to denote its hue, and numbers to denote its value and chroma. For example, scarlet, which is a bright red of medium value is indicated as 5R-5-14. For printers and manufacturers this system is both accurate and practical.

The layman, however, is accustomed to describing color in terms of popular names. This method of course is far less accurate, since many of the traditional color names cover a comparatively wide range of hue, value, and chroma. Pink is used to describe various light shades, such as cherry, coral, rose, shrimp, salmon, peach, apricot, shell, and flesh. Brown is equally indefinite, describing dark shades of tan, walnut, chocolate, cinnamon, tobacco, burnt sienna, sepia, and van dyke.

. . .

* Preface to the *Munsell Book of Color,* published by the Munsell Color Company, Inc., Baltimore, Md., 1929.

It is interesting to notice, when studying the Munsell color samples, that neighboring hues, which when pure, are distinctly different, become almost identical as they approach neutral grey. This is especially true in the darker values, such as Value 4, where Royal purple, magenta, and Chinese red become maroon when sufficiently greyed or neutralized by their complements.

In general, reds, oranges, yellows, and yellow-greens turn into warm grey, while blue-greens, blues, blue-purples, and violets produce cool greys. In the lighter values, 7 and 8, the contrast of warm and cool greys is still noticeable, as "smoke," "mist," and "frost." In darker values the contrast of warm and cool colors suggests sunlight and shadow. This may be the reason why a given landscape may be painted by half a dozen artists in half a dozen color schemes, each of which seems convincing, although no two of them may agree as to actual hues or values. Maxfield Parrish used deep, rich tones; Jules Guerin, light neutral washes. Hence a color composition, like a musical composition, may be transposed into different keys, any one of which may be pleasing in itself, provided that the individual colors, or notes, are in harmony with each other, and with the particular key in which they are painted, or played.

In garden design color compositions are largely determined by the color of the foliage background. Flower colors which seem bright against a deep green look dull against a light yellow-green. Certain flower colors are intensified by purple foliage backgrounds, others by blue-green or silvery grey. This apparent change of hue and chroma may be studied by observing the relative intensity of a few flower colors . . . However, it must be remembered that foliage colors are strongly affected by the texture of the leaf unit, just as blue velvet, which absorbs light, looks darker than the same shade of blue satin, which is so smooth that it reflects light.

Colors that lie opposite each other in [a] circular spectrum chart, are called contrasting or complementary. When mixed together in proper proportions, they complement or neutralize each other. For example, red and blue-green form grey.

Pure colors of strong chroma, used in contrasting or complementary combinations, produce gay and exhilarating effects, as for example—

The flaming orange of sugar maples in autumn against a coerulean [sic] sky.

The pale yellow spikes of thermopsis against deep blue delphinium.

Burnt-orange butterflies hovering over violet-blue asters.

Spring carpets of yellow and purple-blue crocus.

The principles of contrast or opposition remain the same, whether they are applied to shapes and forms, to lines of direction, such as straight and curved, or vertical and horizontal, to complementary colors, or to light and dark values. It is interesting to note, when studying the *Munsell Book of Color,* that whereas bright reds and greens have almost equal values, yellows in their greatest intensities register as light, while the complementary purples and blue-purples are very dark. Hence the greatest color contrast is one of value as well as of hue and chroma. For example—dark purple-blue iris against a light yellow stucco wall.

In garden composition, bright contrasting colors are useful for accent and emphasis, as—

Blue-green junipers against red brick walls.

Yellow-green oriental arborvitae against purple tapestry brick walls.

Although complementary colors enhance each other, the indiscriminate use of too many contrasting colors, whether in a flower border or in an impressionist painting, tends to produce a mottled and muddy effect. This principle was applied during the war to camouflage artillery, by many colors in broken outlines. It can also be demonstrated by fitting discs of colored papers of strong chroma, arranged in proper proportions, upon a top. When the top is spun, the various bright colors merge into grey.

Hence in designing gardens, a heterogeneous mixture of flower colors may result in loss of brilliance, and the general effect appear greyed to the eye.

RESTFUL EFFECTS IN CONTRASTING COLORS

The effect of contrasting colors in dull or neutral tones is more restful than in pure hues, which are bright or intense. For example, a restful color contrast may be obtained by using breeder tulips in various soft shades of yellow with dull blues and dull violets.

Certain flower families contain a complete range of complementary colors in light and dark values, such as the tulips, iris, gladioli, and pansies. In fact, contrasting color combinations are often found in a single flower.

It is always possible to balance a large mass of dull or neutral color with a small amount of vivid complementary color for accent.

In general, backgrounds should be dull, while foreground details may be either dull or bright. This applies to the color scheme of a room, of a costume, or of a garden. Otherwise the background would "jump" into the foreground, as sometimes happens in poorly painted stage scenery.

Fortunately most foliage colors are duller than flower colors, except those varieties known as "aurea," which should not be used as backgrounds. These mustard greens are too intense to serve as anything but ornaments.

Hue and chroma appear to be relative, depending upon the intensity of the colors that surround them. . . .

CLOSELY RELATED COLORS

Colors that lie next [to] each other in the rainbow or spectrum are called neighboring or closely related, as for example, red, orange, yellow.

Vivid color combinations can be produced by using closely related colors of high intensity.

Warm colors range from reds, through oranges and yellows, to yellow-greens. They occur in bright hues in a number of flowers—marigolds, poppies, and nasturtiums.

Cool colors consist of blue-greens, green-blues, blues, purple-blues, and violets. The English language is lacking in adequate words to describe them.

Closely related color schemes are most effective when confined either to warm or cool colors, although sweet peas, hyacinths, lupin [sic], and asters, combine light shades of warm yellows and pinks with light or dark shades of cool violets and blues.

The azaleas, which vary from cerise and magenta, through crimson and scarlet, to orange and yellow, are rather excruciating together, but create pleasing effects when used in smaller groups of neighboring colors, such as magenta, crimson, lilac, and mauve; or flame, bronze, orange, and buff.

Harmonious transitions may be made between two bright hues by the introduction of neighboring colors in neutral tones.

Zinnias are excellent examples, and also chrysanthemums.

White is valuable for separating colors rather than for creating harmonies. It serves as a transition between warm and cool colors in light values, which are often called "pastel tints." When combined with darker values, white flowers become silhouetted, and are especially striking against evergreen backgrounds.

SUBORDINATION TO A DOMINANT HUE

Just as an indoor room is more pleasing when designed about a single color, as the "blue room" or the "gold room," so an outdoor room becomes more striking when the color scheme is confined to one dominant hue. For example, a pool, lined and bordered with bright blue tiles, may serve as the keynote for a garden color scheme. Dull blue foliage walls in light and dark values may be formed by shearing Koster's blue spruce to an even width and height. Neutral tones of blue-grey slate for walks and terraces may be bordered by steel blue edgings of spice pink. Iron furniture may be painted dull blue; while for accent and ornament, pots of blue and purple cabbages may be used.

"Grass green" as a color does not exist. If a bench is painted the color of a grass panel in the early spring, it will clash with the changing greens of the grass all through the season. Foliage greens vary as much as grass greens. They are affected by season, by weather, and by soil. Under adverse conditions the foliage of Scotch pine, which is normally bluish-green, will turn to yellow-green. During droughts, red and purple leaf foliage plants grow sickly green.

In the spring all foliage is lighter in color and finer in texture than in the fall. The new leaves of the ash and the flower buds and twigs of the red maple suggest in early spring the colors of their autumn foliage.

During the winter many evergreens turn bronze, particularly the junipers, cryptomerias, leucothes [sic], andromedas, mahonias, and cotoneasters

. . .

FLOWER PATTERNS

"Disconnected groups of flowers cannot be called compositions."
DOW

Instead of a succession of hit and miss flower color in continuous bloom, it is far more entertaining to arrange a series of flower patterns. Different color schemes may be designed for different seasons upon the same garden plan. For example, spring colors may be used in border patterns . . . ; summer colors in a low center panel with tall spikes at the corners . . . ; and the fall colors again along the borders, with a high mass across the end for a terminal. . . . When trying out flower patterns, it is cheaper to use annual flower seeds than perennial plants, until one is satisfied with the progressive color combinations.

If a few varieties are used in large quantities and are carefully chosen for foliage effect as well as for flower color, the areas not in bloom at any given time will present a pleasing and fairly uniform mass of green.

It is well to remember that perennials do not always bloom on schedule. They vary without notice according to weather and soil conditions. For instance if the spring flowers bloom too late or the summer flowers too early, disastrous results may follow in the color arrangement.

For this reason it is advisable to select a dominant hue

for summer which will fit into both the spring and fall color schemes.

If yellow and orange are chosen for spring; pink and lavender for fall; a keystone of blue, sustained throughout the summer, will complement the yellow and orange, and also harmonize with the lavender and pink.

White can always be used for this purpose, but is less interesting than key colors selected from the color chart.

Yellow, as a dominant hue during the summer, will form a pleasing contrast with spring blue and violet, and also harmonize with autumn orange and bronze.

Crimson, as a dominant summer hue, will harmonize with cerise in the spring, and with scarlet and maroon in the fall.

FLOWER PICTURES

In garden composition, flower colors attract attention and create interest. They may be used in a parterre pattern, like a solid embroidery; or as an ornament, like a centerpiece; or grouped, to form a picture.

The Japanese have a custom of arranging one decoration in their living rooms at a time, and when they have thoroughly enjoyed it, they substitute another. This method can be applied to a small garden by arranging flower pictures to be seem from different points of view at different seasons, as follows—

Near the door; as one enters a cottage garden.

At the corners; as one sits on the porch.

Near the gate; as one leaves the garden.

When designing these pictures, it is well to study the doors, porches, corners, and gates through a small paper finder, made by cutting a square or a rectangular hole in a piece of cardboard. This finder is as useful in determining garden pictures as is the finder of a camera in selecting views for photographs.

The desire for continuous bloom often results in tiresome, spotty effects. . . .

Flower borders should be as carefully designed as flower panels. The same pattern that was used for the border of an Oriental rug, may be used for a border of flowers. This may be a definite, repeated pattern, . . . or a ribbon design . . . Both arrangements provide for a succession of bloom throughout the season.

COLOR SCHEMES

Since flower colors are seasonal or temporary, the permanent color scheme of a garden must depend upon such materials as walls and fences, pavements and surfacing, evergreen backgrounds, borders and ground-covers. . . .

If the garden is to be used only in the summer, deciduous foliage may be considered as part of the underlying scheme.

Unless the garden happens to be far removed from the house, the colors of the house walls, trim, awnings, and other accessories, should be incorporated into the color scheme.

. . .

LIGHT AND DARK VALUES

Every color composition should be studied in terms of light and dark masses.

Consider the garden pattern as a woodblock without color. What is the proportion of dark to light masses in your composition? Which serves as background, as foreground, as accent?

Study the garden views from focal points in black and white silhouettes.

Then restudy the same views in terms of photographs. What supplies the intermediate shades of grey? . . . Remember that yellows are light and warm suggesting sunshine, while violet and blue-purple are cool and suggest shadow, especially when dark.

Translate the garden composition into a number of different color schemes, using tempora [sic] colors or colored papers graded according to Munsell's measured colors. Remember that the texture of building and plant materials will affect their color values, just as the size and shape of their leaves will determine their scale.

Smooth grey flagstone paths reflect light and therefore register as light grey; while rough stone walls of the same color and shade absorb light and so must be considered as medium grey. Green leaves with dull finish also absorb light. Some will register medium grey like the stone wall; others darker grey. This also applies to flowers in neutral shades of medium or dark colors. For accent use flowers and furniture in dark or light values,—dark iron and wood, or light aluminum and rawhide.

Evergreen gardens of yew or box, with medium green panels of turf, and pale green foliage plants with white flowers, are equally handsome in midsummer, or in midwinter after a light snow fall.

Green gardens of light and dark deciduous foliage form handsome frames for distant views, or create dignified settings for public buildings.

Masses of lupin and larkspur may be planted against a white clapboard house with bright blue shutters.

Crimson, rose, and shell pink peonies may be arranged

against a dark background of purple leaf plums and copper beeches.

A buff stone wall serves as an excellent background for climbing roses in shades of copper, gold, and cream.

Whether in complementary or closely related color combinations, light values create delicate harmonies suggesting lavender and old lace; while dark values produce rich and somber effects.

Two contrasting colors in contrasting values produce exquisite effects in parks and gardens. Against the pale silvery green of the Russian olive, corn flowers with silvery foliage and mauve and maroon flowers strike an unusual note in garden compositions; while near a grove of dull blue-green Scotch pines, drifts of California poppies may be broadcast, with pale blue-green foliage and tangerine blossoms.

COLOR PERSPECTIVE

In the landscape, objects at a great distance appear smaller and closer together, and also lighter and greyer because the air screens them like a soft veil.

To create an illusion of distance in a landscape painting, bright colors are used in the foreground, followed by dull tones in progressively lighter values, to soft light greys in the background. Three values are sufficient to produce this effect, especially when combined with converging lines and diminishing sizes, as in the flat washes of a poster.

When applied to foliage and flower colors, the same principle holds true.

A garden theatre on a small property will seem to have great depth if the foreground foliage is of dark green red cedar, the wings of blue-green Chinese juniper, and the background of grey-green silver cedar. Or it could be developed with bright green Siberian arborvitae, dull green American arborvitae, and light yellow-green vervaene arborvitae.

A pageant green on a much larger scale would require larger trees, such as spruce, fir, or pine. For foreground foliage, the rich green Austrian pine with its coarse needles could be used; for wing planting, the dull green, finer foliage of white pine; and for background, the soft grey tassels of the bhotan or Himalayan pine.

A rose garden may be arranged with bright reds in the foreground, shading to light pinks in the background, as follows: crimson, cherry red, bright rose, old rose, pale rose, shell pink, and pearl white; or scarlet, coral, shrimp pink, salmon, peach, flesh, and ivory white.

A perennial border may be arranged in contrasting colors to create an illusion of distance, by using—

Royal blue and Canary Yellow

China Blue and Lemon Yellow

Ash Blue and Sulphur Yellow

The wide range of colors available in tulips allow for many combinations of hue, value, and chroma. An harmonious color scheme, to produce an effect of distance, may be secured by planting bands of closely related colors from foreground to background, in the following order—

Deep Violet with Mulberry and Wine Red

Heliotrope with Raspberry and Strawberry

Amethyst with Mauve and Taupe

Lavender with Light Mauve and Old Rose

Pale Lavenders and Shell Pinks

Silvery Lavender and Pearl Grey

BEATRIX JONES FARRAND
(1872–1959)

*Although most designers agree on the importance of
thoughtful long-term maintenance in order to preserve
design intention, it is unusual for a landscape gardener to
prepare extensive maintenance notes. Beatrix Farrand
prepared these notes for the Dumbarton Oaks gardeners
in the late '40s after the property was transferred from
the private ownership of Robert Words and Mildred
Barnes Bliss to the institutional ownership
of Harvard University.*

BEATRIX FARRAND'S PLANT BOOK
FOR DUMBARTON OAKS

The Rose Garden
. . .

This is the largest of the terraces in the Dumbarton Oaks garden plan. As the gardens were always thought likely to be much seen in winter, the thought behind the planting of the Rose Garden has been given quite as much to the evergreen and enduring outlines and form as to the Roses, which, at their season, give added charm to this level. The Roses in the Rose Garden are really only secondary to the general design of the garden and its form and mass. The high wall, on the west side with its latticed-brick balustrade, shows the difference in the material thought appropriate to use on account of the added distance from the house and its more formal lines. The high wall is made of stone, with pilasters of brick, interrupted into panels. The pilasters of brick support the upper lattice-brick wall, which makes the parapet to the Box Terrace. This high wall is an admirable place on which to grow certain climbing Roses, perhaps a *Magnolia grandiflora, Clematis paniculata,* and a wispy veil of *Forsythia suspensa* narrowing the steps leading from the Box to the Rose Garden Terrace.

Big accent Box are used at the entrance steps, and there should be one large clipped Box in the middle of the garden, and probably four more large ones in two each of

Source: Washington, D.C.: Dumbarton Oaks, Trustees for Harvard University, 1980. Edited by Diane Kostial McGuire.

the north and south beds. These tall Box are intended for winter accent and as foils to the Roses growing alongside them. It is recognized that they are bad neighbors to the Roses, but this disadvantage must be taken into account when the general effect of the year is considered as a whole. Accent Box are also needed in comparatively small size at both the north and the south gates, and at the opening of the steps on the east side of the garden leading toward the Fountain Terrace.

The edgings to the Rose beds should also be of Box— *suffruticosa* of varying heights—and no bed border should be allowed to grow too tall. If the Box borders to the beds are allowed to grow too large, the whole terrace becomes dwarfed and becomes a series of Box-enclosed and almost invisible beds. Therefore, the Box edgings must be replaced, perhaps over fifteen or twenty years.

The center plant in the garden may be allowed to grow to a considerable height, perhaps even fifteen feet, but the designer feels that the marker plants should be distinctly secondary in size, in order not to overwhelm the iron gates at the north and south entrances to the garden or to so dominate the garden that the Roses are hardly noticed.

In choosing the colors for the Roses in general, the pink and salmon color-sorts have been selected for the second third, together with a few of the very deep red ones, such as Etoile de Hollande and Ami Quinard. The center third of the garden was planted more particularly with salmon-colored and yellowish pink Roses, while the northern third was given over entirely to yellow or predominantly yellow and orange sorts.

The beds surrounding these center, formal beds have been used for small bush Roses, such as the *polyantha,* some of the hybrid singles, and some of the smaller species Roses. The climbing Roses grown on the west wall have included

Mermaid, Silver Moon, Dr. Van Fleet, American Pillar, Reveil Dijonnais, and Cl. Frau Karl Druschki.

. . .

The Fountain Terrace

. . .

This terrace is the one real flower garden in the series of terraces sloping eastward from the main building. In the spring, probably the best bulbs to use will be Tulips, in such colors as may be found attractive. The cheapest groups which can be bought in large quantities are those of the mixed Darwins, preferably running toward the yellows, bronzes, and oranges, but if these colors prove difficult to find, the old-fashioned rainbow mixture of all sorts of colors can wisely be substituted. It should be insisted that the tulips be supplied of sorts approximately of even height, and all of late-blooming varieties, as "misses" in the border where early-flowering Tulips come and go before the rest of the plantations are in bloom, make decided blanks in the composition. Under the Tulips, and making a border for them, annuals such as Forget-me-not, Pansies, Daisies, and possibly *Arabis,* may be set out. This garden is the one in which most change and replacement is necessary, in order to keep up the blooming effect throughout the season, and any alteration in the scheme permitting this blooming effect throughout the season would seem a mistaken economy. The area planted to the revolving series of flowers is a comparatively small one, and therefore not much space is required for propagation. After the Tulips have finished their blooming, summer-flowering annuals are planted in the borders; in the past, yellows, bronzes, blues, and primrose shades have been found attractive, rather than shades of pink, lavender, or crimson. The autumn display on this terrace for the last years, has been an effective grouping of yellow Chrysanthemums in various shades, with bronze, deep brown, and maroon, but no pinks or whites have worked in well with this scheme of color. If the Herbaceous Border is kept up, the pink, lavender, and purple Tulips, the pink and white and lavender summer flowers, and more white Chrysanthemums may be used than on the Fountain Terrace.

The wall on the west side of the Fountain Terrace again reveals the sharp drop in level between the Rose Garden and the level of the terrace itself. Here again, the steps have been broken into three different flights in order to make the climbing not too laborious a process. Two-thirds of the way down the steps, a seat, under a lead canopy, is placed on the landing, and when possible, is surrounded by pot plants which harmonize in color with those used in the garden.

Outside the east wall of the Fountain Terrace, Kieffer Pear trees are planted in an almost solid hedge that also stretches along the north wall. This hedge is, again, planted as a support to the garden, which otherwise would be obviously hanging over retreating grades and suspended unpleasantly in the air. The great beauty of the planting outside the east wall is a magnificent English Beech (*Fagus sylvatica Riversii*) of the darkest shade. Under this, a group of spring-flowering bulbs used to be planted—such as *Leucojum aestivum*, Aconite, and *Scilla nutans** in its different shades—and later-flowering *Tiarella* and some Maidenhair and other ferns. If it be not possible to keep up this border with its formal planting, a carpet of Ivy would be easy to maintain. A plant or two of Clematis, Ivy, and fine-leaved *Parthenocissus Lowii* clothe the wall but do not cover it completely.

On the west wall, on either side of the big flight of steps, *Parthenocissus heterophylla* should be allowed to cover this area,

* Hortus Third: *Endymion non-scriptus*

and to cover the heavy wall enclosing the steps, as this wall, if unclothed, is overmassive in its scale.

Two espaliered *Magnolia grandiflora* may be used, if not too large, in matching positions on the east side of the west wall; and two fine plants of *Taxus cuspidata* should also be used at the back of the west borders, both to clothe and hide the heavy wall and to reduce the size of the border.

Outside the terrace on the southwest, a group of flowering Dogwood (*Cornus florida*) should be kept constantly replaced, as this feature tends to offset what is again a difficult alteration in level, and to give interest and flower in spring as well as fruit and color in autumn.

The south gate in the new, south, stone wall is marked by clipped plants of American Holly (*Ilex opaca*) at either side. These should not be allowed to become too large, as the garden is of such small size that a heavy pair of plants would throw it out of balance. The south walk is aimed almost immediately at an Apple tree which has been doctored and fed to keep it in good condition. When it fails, it should be replaced by a fair-size tree, as the effect of the rounded top and the blossomed branches, as seen from the south side of the Fountain Terrace, is a valuable part of the composition.

The transition from the brick walks of the Beech Terrace to the flagged walks of the Rose Garden and again to the grass walks of the Fountain Terrace has all been carefully thought out, and, as there is no "gangway" either from east to west or from north to south on this terrace, it should be possible to keep the turf in good condition. Two fountains are kept filled and playing during the summer season, and it is important that their curbs be allowed to become as mossy as possible, as, scrubbed and cleaned well, the curbs would look new and fresh and garish, whereas the fountains should appear to have been "found" there and to be a part of the old plan.

GARRETT ECKBO
(b. 1910)

Landscape for Living, *published in 1950, is the seminal
book for modern American landscape architecture. Its
freshness of approach and attention to detail, which have
always characterized Eckbo's design, work as well and are as
valid today as they were forty years ago. Eckbo has been
deeply interested in the role of plants in landscape design,
and he has used them with significant success, where plants
and architectural structure complement one another in a
dynamic manner. In this way, his work parallels that of
Luis Barragan in Mexico and Roberto Burle Marx
in Brazil.*

LANDSCAPE FOR LIVING

Anti-Gravity Materials: Plants and Planting

Many many volumes of poetry and of poetic prose have been written about plants and planting. Some of this has been well-written, some badly written; some beautiful, some corny. We are in agreement with the intentions of all these writers. Plants are endlessly fascinating: endlessly gracious, endlessly lovely, endlessly strong, persistent and adaptable, magnificent and fragile, colorful and variable, rich in structure and form, color and texture, architectural and sculptural and natural all at once, filled with potentiality for the free harmony of a beautiful world.

With the consideration of plants in the landscape we leave the ground plane, the floor of our garden space, to which earth, rock, and water are unbreakably bound however they may be carved and moulded and constructed, however ruggedly and picturesquely arranged by man or nature. The larger plants live with us the people IN the air space of the landscape, resisting and eluding gravity in the upward aspiration of their growth, yet firmly anchored, with their roots entrenched in the solid earthbound mantle rock. The plants live in space and in the earth at once, and each and every plant is in itself an organization of space, containing within its three-dimensional silhouette a most complex and variable enclosure, a structure of marvelous articulation and delicacy, a piece of constructivist sculpture of the most tre-

Source: [New York]: F. W. Dodge Corporation, 1950.

mendous richness in variety, ranging in scale from the microcosm of the moss clump to the macrocosm of the great tropical banyan tree. Earth, rock and water are bound by gravity; plants defy it; that is the essense [sic] of space sensation, one reason for our love and need for plants.

Every plant, even of the prostrate or clinging kinds, is a study in most delicate equilibrium, in a most harmonious adjustment of many parts to meet the needs of the whole. The root structure, spreading or deep below ground, balances in cubic volume the vegetative structure above ground. It anchors the plant in one place, and forms that firm yet flexible base from which the upper parts defy gravity and the vagaries and violences of the weather. From this firm clutch upon the bosom of mother earth the plant reaches toward light and air in balanced radial symmetry, often distorted by weather, site or other plants, but always in balance, always a display of the fantastically endless variety of biological constructivism, more delicate, elegant, flexible, sturdy, or massive than man has yet produced. Upon this lithe and tenacious structure, with its permanent or changing costuming in all the manifold richness of foliage—the primary food-producing element of the plant—are borne, seasonally, intermittently, or constantly, the reproductive elements, the flowers and fruit, that collection of delicately articulated jewels of unparalleled variety in form, color, and texture, which has been one of the chief delights and pursuits of gardeners since man first settled down on the land.

As design material plants are kinetic, not static. A plant is a living, growing structure, a unit of life. From the quick annual wild flower in the desert to the mighty redwoods and big trees which antedate the Christian church, every plant changes in form and aspect from day to day or from season to season. Plants are the bridge from inert matter to organic life, the spark plug in the great life-cycle of water, soil, plants and animals. The process of photosynthesis carried on by the chlorophyll in the plants of the world is its basic production relation, basic to the growth of the landscape, basic to the animal kingdom, basic to the societies of man. Our "ornamental" planting—our shade trees and hedges and flowers, our cacti and succulents and alpines, our bog gardens and aquatics, our lawns and meadows—as it functions in forming and enriching the spaces in which we live, is at the same time symbolic to us of the wild life-cycle of primeval nature, and of the organized life-cycle of human agriculture. The productive force of green growth, and the reproductive force of flower and fruit, as given sensitive, esthetic expression in our gardens and parks, is the very essence of the basic vitality of nature, that nature which is the world we live in, and which we are ourselves.

. . .

Structure is thought of as THE art of spatial design, but planting is likewise an art of spatial design—the primary spatial control out-of-doors, equal qualitatively to structural design, though varying in kind; that is subtler, looser, less positive, less continuous, or with wider variations in degree of continuity. To speak of color first, texture second, and mass third, as does Robinson, is not only to reverse the scale of importance, to stand values on their heads, but also to ignore the primary spatial essence of plants.* Every plant, no matter how low, how prostrate, how massive, matted, or solidly bushy, how fastigiate or billowing, is nevertheless a construction in space and an enclosure of space. As we go up in the scale of space organization, from the grass, ground covers, herbaceous material and vines which are primarily surfacing or enriching elements, to the shrubs and trees which

* Robinson, William (1838–1935). Prolific author and editor, famous for promoting natural garden styles over formal ones. Author of many books including *The Wild Garden* and *The English Flower Garden*.

are the real enclosing and sheltering forms, this spatial quality becomes, of course, more obvious and more important. To stress color, texture, and mass is to concede that planting is merely decorative, to endeavor to make it into a kind of sculpture or painting which it is not, to relapse into the search for pictures and miss the great lyric opportunities of landscape design.

Plant material, as an aggregation of units of unlimited variety in form, size, color, and texture, has esthetic possibilities which have scarcely been scratched. The variety and richness of plants as a material for creative organization are limited only by questions of culture and maintenance, and by the scope and freedom of the plan conception. We are offered a richness of vocabulary, a wealth of palette, not surpassed by the material range of any other sort of creative work. This variety proposes a problem of discipline in selection which is difficult to achieve. But the ingredients of this discipline are to be found in the problems of culture and maintenance, and in the need for development of a new and more dynamic esthetic of plant arrangement in relation to site-space form. Planting design is primarily the grouping of a number of forms, varying in size and proportions, in a three-dimensional arrangement. Within this grouping there can be formal and space relations comparable, in degree but not in kind, to those in sculpture and painting.

Most planting is done practically, pictorially, sentimentally and/or commercially. Practically to solve such problems as ground cover, erosion control, windbreaks, screens, shade, et cetera; pictorially to provide "pictures to look at" (the terminal feature, the garden vista, the naturalistic glade, all heavily propagandized in professional and amateur garden publications); sentimentally to recall an emotion (the rock garden, the old-fashioned garden, the bog garden, the English garden); and commercially to move nursery stock (foundation planting is a standard technique). These objectives are all valid when properly interpreted in relation to the planning problems which exist; without such relation they become fragmentary or irrelevant. The usual concentration on them tends to minimize or overlook the tremendous potential for symphonic spatial experience latent in landscape design. This potential has scarcely been scratched in our times, save in a few great parks and estates. It has been foreshadowed in some of the great historic gardens, in some of the unconsciously dynamic planting carried out in the rural countryside, and in such natural features as meadows and groves of trees. But it has yet to be exploited consciously, boldly, and with the full sweep of man's creative imagination, allied with the rich variety of free natural growth.

. . .

FORM

As we go further into the detail of plant forms their richness in variety expands rapidly. The variations in ultimate dimensions, in height and spread and rate of growth, become simplicity itself when we consider the fantastic variability in general form and structure within the ornamental plant world. With the circular (unless distorted by external factors) plan[t] form of the single unit as a common denominator, we have a range of form in elevation from those which are horizontal in the proportion of as much as one unit high to ten or twelve spread, through every imaginable intermediate variation to those which are vertical in the proportion of one unit of spread to as many as ten high. Structural forms go through all variations of symmetry and irregularity. From horizontality to verticality, from regularity to irregularity, from symmetry to contortion, from rigidity to pliability, from erection to prostration, from climbing to crawling, from the open tracery to the dense mass, the variation is endless. (We can speak of plants which are traceries, and of plants which are massive, but we must remember that no plant, save such occasional specializations as the barrel cactus, is in its overall relations a mass.) In relation of three-dimensional silhouette to supporting structure, and in relation of these to size and rate of growth, the variability becomes so complex as to get beyond rationalization or classification. We can list among trees the round-headed, the spreading, the irregular, the vertical oval, the slender upright, the fastigiate, the vertical with horizontal branches, and so on. But to further break these down into all the angular and curving, regular and irregular, opposite and alternate relations of twig to branch to trunk becomes a task for a future academy of plant design with research resources beyond any existing. This is perhaps the point at which the rational becomes irrational, the objective subjective, and the scientific artistic.

Most trees take one form when they are young, another as they mature, and a third as they grow old. Shrubs, too, change character with maturity. Especially the larger and more erect species tend to open up and lose their lower branches, becoming quasi-tree forms. This tendency is subject to considerable control by pruning. Most permanent shrub and vine forms tend to develop woody lower structures of considerable character and interest, comparable to trees, as they mature and age. Design can take advantage of this tendency rather than foster the frantic gardening efforts to conceal legs and stems.

To speak of natural form is incomplete—we must ask, natural form where? under what conditions? The single pine in the open meadow, the pine crowded with many others in a dense grove, the pine on exposed mountain top or sea shore, will scarcely be recognizable as the same species. We must establish a relation between the visualization of a certain kind of form, the selection of a kind which tends to develop in that direction, and the creation of conditions which will encourage it. This is what we mean by collaboration between material and artist.

TEXTURE

From variations in structure and silhouette to variations in texture is a step from complexity to infinity. It is from this relation between foliage and structure that most of us recognize and identify plants as they are generally used in landscape design, rather than from the more scientific procedures of botanical taxonomy. This is particularly true of the larger material, the woody and semi-woody shrubs and trees, the sizable herbaceous material, the climbers, trailers, and sprawlers.

In size foliage ranges from the tiny scales of heather and juniper, through all the intermediate variations of "ordinary" garden plants, to the startling extremes of Magnolia triflora [sic], palms, elephant ears, gunnera, and philodendron. In form foliage can be classified in a range typified by linear (pine needles), lanceolate (lance-shaped), ovate (oval), obovate (fat oval), cordate (heart-shaped), and so on. Complicating these are intermediates (linear-lanceolate, cordate-obovate); variations from symmetry in the individual leaf; variations in the edge (simple, toothed, holly-like, lobed) and in the point; special forms; variations in thickness and stiffness, and varying combinations of these (thick-soft, thin-stiff); variations in veining; variations in pinnation, that is, dissection of the leaf into a few or many smaller leaflets; variations in the texture of each leaf (smooth-glossy, smooth-dull, fuzzy, crinkled, etc.); variations in the length and angle of the petiole connecting leaf to twig or stem; and so on. The variation in foliage, like the variation in rocks, is endless and endlessly fascinating. Unlike rocks, it has been difficult to preserve, save in the dusty pages of the herbarium. Plant specimens can now be preserved intact in cold poured transparent plastic blocks, and we can look forward to the day when such a library will be part of every school of landscape design.

Each step in variation in plant form is a multiple variation by virtue of its cross-reference with all the previous variations. Thus the progression in complexity is geometric rather than arithmetic. In foliage arrangement, as related to plant structure, we have further wide variation: from thin-scattered to dense-crowded, from even-all-over-the-plant to grouped-in-bunches-or-tufts, from erect through horizontal to pendant, from stiff to pliable to tremulous, from sprinkles through fronds to clumps, the range can scarcely be catalogued. Consider these in relation to variations in leaf form, leaf size, plant structure (producing silhouette), size and rate of growth, as well as color, and the limitless richness of the plant palette becomes increasingly obvious.

A further most important variation in the textural quality of plants appears in those which are deciduous, that is, which develop a permanent woody structure but lose their leaves in winter. The great virtue, richness and interest of deciduous plants lies precisely in those continuous seasonal changes which are associated in so many minds with the cold and storms of eastern winters. "They look so dead." From the fresh light greens and bronzes of bursting spring, through the rich mature greens of summer and the gorgeous reds, browns and yellows of fall, to the complete exposure of trunk, branch, and stem structure in all their elegance, strength, refinement or fantasy during the winter, deciduous trees, shrubs, and vines put on a continuous show which is not to be matched for variety and interest by any of the

evergreen plants save perhaps those with showy flowers. There is a kind of cultural lag expressed in our typical concentration on greenery and flowers, to the exclusion of interest in structure and texture. We don't have to reject any of these; rather it is necessary to include them all to rescue our landscapes from dull and mechanical design.

Plants can be classified as foliage plants if the leafage covers the structural parts, as structural plants if they are exposed and dominant in character, as both if the two tend to balance, as in many trees. Some trees may be foliage plants from the outside, and structural when one goes under and within them—as olives and avocados. Some may be foliage in summer and structural in winter.

Another aspect of the relation between foliage and structure in trees, with considerable bearing on their location, is the following:

> The only power of motion possessed by a tree lies in its growth upward, downward, and outward. It is capable of being moved, however, and the great mover is the wind. . . .
> VAN DYKE

COLOR

We come then at last to color. It can be said that American gardens (English gardens? French gardens?) are color-happy. This is not to depreciate the value of color, which makes the world understandable, vibrant, and magnificent for us. But color, in its purer and stronger forms, comes in our world in fractional quantities, save for special or seasonal bursts, within a general framework of greens, browns, and blues, each grayed with some admixture of the other and with the changes in light and atmosphere relations. The

purer and stronger the color we introduce, the more carefully considered must be its quantity, and its relations with
other colors and elements around it. The "riot of color," that
romantic vision of the garden beautiful, is too often, like
"informal design," merely an excuse for sloppy, haphazard,
irresponsible planting. We advocate the use of color, but we
advocate its use in a disciplined and controlled fashion which
will strengthen, rather than disrupt, the spatial concept of
garden or park.

Color in plants is normally thought of as flower or fruit
color, because those are the most striking. But foliage and
structure likewise have color, of considerable range: in foliage
from gray, blue-gray, and brown-gray through gray-green,
light, medium, and dark green, to various purple and red
shades, not to mention variegations of silver, yellow, and red;
from the lightness of Russian olive and silver poplar to the
darkness of evergreen, magnolia, avocado, purple plum, or
copper beech; in bark from the white birch through many dull
grays and browns, to the reds of madrone and manzanita and
some near blacks, such as the Australian ironback. These colors are generally grayed and toned down by contrast with the
clarity of flower and fruit colors. They are also subject to considerable variation under varying conditions of soil, atmosphere, cultivation, climate, and season. Even some of the
evergreens have considerable seasonal variations: the myrtle
family has noticeably bronze or gray young growth; Chinese
photinia and sweet viburnum sport occasional bright red
leaves in fall and winter; the plume cypress (Japanese) and
one variety of prostrate common juniper turn respectively
rich bronze and rich purple with winter. Color and texture are
brought out by order and clarity in the development of contrasts of varying degrees of strength and proportion. We can
have a limited symphony in light and dark greens, or we can
have a strong symphony in near-blacks and -whites. The lim-

ited symphony can, of course, have its seasonal crescendos of red and yellow foliage, or pink and white blossoms.

There is a climatic or zonal relation of these colors, particularly in foliage. The strong clear greens and variegations seem to be produced by the positive ecological zones, the humid tropical and temperate forests. As we move into the negative zones of heat and aridity or frigidity the foliage colors in trees and shrubs tend toward grays, gray-greens, brown-greens, and the general landscape quality becomes thinner, paler, browner or grayer. Likewise textures seem to vary zonally: the fine glossy surfaces develop in the positive zones, the dull and fuzzy ones in the negative zones where they are protective coverings.

This is where the function of man as equalizer of his environment comes in. In the positive zones, particularly where the humidity rises to the point of discomfort (as in the tropics), or where coolness and fog prevail (as our northwest coast), the darker, heavier, and glossier greens, which are most at home in such climates, tend to accentuate the oppressive or discomforting qualities of the atmosphere. Here we are apt to encourage the lighter, clearer greens, the thinner forms in cool zones, and even silver and gold variegations in zones where the atmosphere is dull and dark. In the negative zones, on the other hand, where light, heat, and dryness press upon us, we tend to promote the growth of the darker, brighter, glossier, or clearer greens, the larger and richer foliage which feels cool and moist. This we do by artificially increasing the humidity, i.e. by irrigation. Thus we seek two values in every landscape: one, the expression of the native quality of the landscape, the other, the development of maximum human livability. The latter is the equalizing value, but it is not incompatible with the former, except in the old-fashioned mystical formulation which makes man subservient to nature.

The relation of atmosphere and light to landscape design has a more specific relation to planting design. The above climatic zones are distinguished by variations in these qualities: the bright humidity of the tropics, the dull humidity of the cool coastal zones, the harsh brightness of the desert, the myriad atmospheric variations of the humid temperate east. . . .

We must design with plant form, texture and color, partly in relation to general and local natural ecology—"most plants are green"—and partly in relation to a scientific evaluation of maximum human livability. Even as there is a developing science of indoor color, concerned with psychological reactions, so there can be a science of outdoor color and texture, concerned with such things as the oppressive quality of the dark heavy tree, the cheering quality of the light sparkling tree. If our landscape conception calls for a grove of copper beeches, perhaps contrasted with a block of silver box elders, the former related to a larger background of light clear greens, the latter to dark heavy greens, we will not seek justifying precedent in wild nature, but only in our own imaginative appraisal of the given situation. We must evaluate form, texture, and color in terms of their effect on the general outdoor space which is being developed, rather than in terms of how "natural" they are, or what illusions or pictures they may create.

Flowers and fruit must be considered in two relations—one, on the plant which bears them, and two, cut and arranged in containers in the house. Flower arrangement is a rich and fascinating art in its own right; it is a kind of microcosm of decorative planting design, without either the cultural problems or the potential permanence of the latter. We will not attempt to consider it here. Flowers grown in the garden should first be separated as to whether they are primarily to be seen there, or to be cut for house use. The latter are difficult, though not impossible to use in the garden scheme: maintenance procedures are apt to be simplified if they are grown in functional rows in the work space or service yard. This applies to all those, such as hybrid tea roses, whose principal asset is their flowers, and to those, such as many annuals, which require steady care and frequent changing to keep them looking good.

We are concerned primarily, then, with flowers and fruit on plants in the garden or park, and hence with the size and form of those plants which produce showy color in these reproductive parts. We can separate first the woody plants from those which are herbaceous. The latter include the general run of garden annuals and perennials, bulbs, alpines, bog plants, aquatics, succulents, annual and perennial vines, and so on. This herbaceous material is in general smaller—below eye level—more seasonal, and less permanent than the woody material. There are exceptions to each—large size, continuity of effect, long life and persistence—but seldom all three in the same plant. Thus there are large annuals and biennials—sun flowers, hollyhocks—which are persistent by seeding themselves, but in unexpected places. There are perennials, bulbs, succulents which are quite persistent with proper care, but which come and go with the seasons. Morning-glories will cover considerable areas, but disappear each winter, and so on.

This herbaceous material we must consider, in general, as being enriching—rather than surfacing, enclosing, or sheltering—material in the landscape scheme. This means that it must play its part within a spatial framework of greater continuity and reliability. With that framework once well established, the herbaceous material can be woven in either incidentally, to satisfy horticultural interests and ambitions, or in carefully interlocked spatial relations, whereby a sizeable block of low but strong color can play a dominant role in the spatial harmony. The danger is, of course, that we may plan for the incidental first, and get something with the strength of the second, with disruptive and disharmonious results. The place of this herbaceous material in the general theory of landscape design, when we cannot establish sure control of its use, comes within an inevitable and quite desirable category of unplanned, accidental, possibly disruptive, but highly vital design elements. The really disruptive or overpowering herbaceous forms are few in number; most of them are subject to easy inclusion within a relatively permanent and dominant background framework. Seasonal bursts of color—as the daffodils in spring or the chrysanthemums in fall—can play the role of seasonal dominance of herbaceous societies in grassland climaxes.

Climatic regionalism is relevant to the selection and use of herbaceous material. In temperate Europe Baroque parterres and Victorian carpet-bedding climaxed in the English wild garden and herbaceous border, those crowning achievements of Robinson and Jekyll* since become English institutions. The greater extremes of the temperate eastern U. S. makes the herbaceous border more difficult, but still possible. In the semi-arid and arid climates it becomes a struggle and a test of caretakers' skill and faithfulness. In these climates for color we tend to fall back on such reliable and hardy elements as geraniums, lantana, the larger bulbs, and succulents. Certain persistent annuals and perennials tend to acclimatize themselves, too—hollyhock, alyssum, nasturtium, coreopsis, morning-glory. In tropical Brazil, in the rich and flamboyant work of Roberto Burle Marx, painter turned landscape gardener, working with the pinks and purples, the fantastic forms and textures, of tropical plant material, we

* Jekyll, Gertrude (1843–1932). Author and garden designer, disciple of William Robinson. Known for her long and elaborate herbaceous borders, which had carefully graduated color schemes.—Ed.

find coming to great fruition in a new cultural climate the separate but analogous traditions of Chinese-Japanese painter-landscaper and English herbaceous romanticism.

The woody plants, being the more durable forms which are able to survive extremes of cold, heat, drought, or neglect, are the primary structural plant forms in the garden, those which can be relied on, together with earth, rock, and construction, to establish a reliable spatial framework within which the active and varied counterpoint of seasonal herbaceous material, as part of general human living activities, can play. Woody plants, too, produce showy color: from the spring blossoms and fall foliage of the east, through the camellias, rhododendrons, and berried pyracantha and cotoneaster of the west coast, the magnolia and crepe myrtle of the deep south, to the hibiscus, oleander, and trumpet vines of the semi-arid or subtropical southwest. Most such color is strictly seasonal; it is only in the far southwest and southeast that woody plants blooming continuously, intermittently, or for long seasons are common.

As plants get larger and more permanent they must be selected more carefully for specific situations. We can plant anything we want to experiment with in our seasonal borders without great loss in time or money. There we can play with pure color to our heart's content. But with five-year shrubs and twenty-year trees we must be more judicious; we must consider not only the color they can produce for us, but the full size, the rate of growth, the form and structure, the texture, whether deciduous or evergreen, and so on. The tree which is good for summer shade and winter sun, the shrub which will give us enclosure and privacy, may not also be the kind to produce flowers and/or fruit for us. Other things being equal, we can certainly tend to choose those trees and shrubs which give us also some strong seasonal color, in flowers, fruit or foliage. But the other things are seldom equal. The flowering trees are apt to be too small for shade (in which case they can of course be fitted in more incidentally), too evergreen for the winter, too subject to pests and diseases, too messy for the neat garden-housekeeper, and so on. Flower and fruiting shrubs seem, in general, to tend toward an open, loose, irregular or arching habit which makes them useless for screening or solid enclosure. Consider the forms of lilac, mock orange, bridal wreath, hibiscus, cotoneaster, pyracantha. Those ingenious characters who turn to the hedge shears at this point are merely going to ruin good shrubs to make a bad screen. While these remarks are not by any means one hundred percent true (since there are flowering shrubs such as the oleander, which make good durable screens; flowering trees such as the jacaranda and yellow wood, which are good for garden shade; fruiting trees such as the apricot, the fig, and the chestnut, which are likewise good shade), nevertheless they are sufficiently true to reinforce our emphasis on the selection of plants for specific situations ON PLAN, in terms of size, form, texture and color in that order. We do not have to follow the Japanese and concentrate our interest on the form and foliage of plants, nor do we have to follow the garden clubs and concentrate our interest on flowers: we can have both, with adequate imaginative flexibility in our planning.

On the limitless fascination in form and color of flowers and fruit, both ornamental and edible, we need hardly elaborate. Better poets than we have given us lyric and delicately subtle word-evaluations, and the great horticulturists and gardeners of our times have concentrated their energies on the production of constantly improved varieties, larger, more double, brighter, and clearer. If we were to raise a still small voice it might only be to wonder if sometimes the flower doesn't run away with the plant, as in the proliferation of hybrid tea roses. But that is a matter of a general climate of opinion. As long as most of us think that lovely flowers and fruits are the peak product of the garden, its *pièce de résistance*—as indeed they are—those who sell us our plants will continue to breed for flowers and fruits primarily. As we become convinced that this *pièce de résistance* demands an appropriate environment, a suitable setting, a strong spatial framework which will carry on for it when its burst of creation is done; so will the horticulturists and nurserymen concentrate on form, structure and texture as well as flowers. This, of course, they do to a considerable extent today.

The colors of flowers and fruits, especially the herbaceous material, run the gamut. The complex delights of planning the perennial border for all seasons and all color relations have been explored for us in endless garden books and manuals. True blues, especially in deeper and stronger shades, are the choicest and most scarce colors in flower and fruit. Otherwise the general range, through red, pink, yellow, orange, lavender, purple, and white, with all imaginable intermediate variations, is well known and often described. The subtle variations—as pure pink which is merely pale red, carmine pink which has blue in it, salmon pink which has yellow in it—are subject to subtle and delicate handling even as the oils and water colors of the painter's palette. While we occasionally see color combinations which make us somewhat seasick, we are inclined to be skeptical of academic systems. We think stronger and more contrasting color combinations than those normally considered "good taste" are perfectly good and reasonable, and that such combinations are somewhat like food: it's a question of what you have been educated to and are used to. A new food can be examined, sampled, and finally assimilated if we are flexible enough to get over our fixed preconceptions. Those who condemn certain color schemes as "Mexican," "primitive," or "vulgar" are merely guilty of self-sterilization. Those who go to the Mediterranean in search of local color are really in search of humanity.

Design in the pure color relations of paint or flowers is a kind of highly specialized and sensitized department of the general categories of space and object design. In general landscape or architectural practice it becomes a special detail which can be minimized or exaggerated according to individual taste. As we move toward the clear and rich spatial order out-of-doors which we have been discussing, we are sure to need such special detail to complete, intensify and subtilize our big conceptions. At this sitting it seems generally safe to say that those colors having some content of the general landscape colors—brown, green, blue—are best in exposed quantities, while those of more primary or synthetic quality should be held to smaller quantities and more specially planned locations and relations to other colors. In the language of Munsell, hues become safer or less disruptive, in quantity as they become lighter or darker in value and weaker in chroma. [For more on Munsell's color charts, see Marjorie Sewell Cautley's entry, page 133.—Ed.] Clearer values and stronger chromas can be used, with greater care in their quantitative and qualitative relations and in their known psychological reactions on the observer.

. . . In 1908 Frank Lloyd Wright said "Simplicity and repose are qualities that measure the true value of any work of art. . . . But simplicity is not in itself an end nor is it a matter of the side of a barn but rather an entity with a graceful beauty in itself from which discord, and all that is meaningless, has been eliminated. A wild flower is truly simple. . . ." Simplicity can be organized from any number of elements; it is merely more difficult as the number increases.

The relation between the wealth of variety in the plant palette and its analysis in terms of size, form, texture and color points the way to endless systems, of varying complexity and subtlety, for the achievement of unity. The length of the plant list is quite irrelevant to the determination of whether or not this has been achieved. Three badly-selected plants can produce cacophony, fifty well-selected plants a symphony, in the same volume of space. The plant list must first be analyzed in relation to the size (cubage) of the area to be planted. Thereafter it must be analyzed in terms of size, form, color, and texture, and of quantities of each kind of each. Thus we can have a unity by size: one or a few kinds of larger trees or shrubs can dominate and unify many more kinds of smaller woody or herbaceous plants. Variety decreases as we go up the size-scale, increases as we go down. We can have unity by form: stronger forms, as the fastigiate or the weeping, may establish a dominant framework for a variety of looser forms. We can have unity by texture: the large-dark-glossy or the thin-light-fine may predominate throughout one size of plants, or through several sizes. Likewise we can have unity by color. The relations by combination among these patterns for unity become endlessly varied; the only comparable arts are those of sound—music—or of color—painting.

The patterns of unity must be related to spatial eye-level patterns. There is a ground-cover pattern, of grass, herbaceous materials, and low woody planting, as related to inorganic surfacing. There is an eye-level pattern of tall herbs and grasses, medium and tall shrubs, and small trees, as related to structural enclosures. Finally there is an overhead pattern of tree structure and foliage, as related to constructed shelters, and the sky. These patterns can be unified within and/or among themselves.

The standard theory that cost increases with length of plant list is quite unfounded in fact. Prices on the great bulk of nursery stock run quite closely together for similar sizes and conditions of plants; only a few kinds fall at the extremes of cheapness or expensiveness. The contractor who is primarily interested in getting his money and getting off the job may whittle the price a little if he has fewer kinds to locate, but this seldom affects the overall cost greatly, on jobs of any size. It is one thing to meet the necessity of a programmed budget; that is part of the designer's responsibility. It is another thing to design in assumed cost differentials of a few cents or dollars, when that means whittling the quality of the job. In America, the richest country in the world, our design approaches are in the majority poverty-stricken (they call it "economy of means") by pressure of budget, or general "business-like" atmosphere. Who benefits from it? We all have to live in this environment we are sterilizing so persistently by design.

NATIVES

One aspect of selection, which has considerable connection with maintenance, is the relation between native or indigenous and foreign or exotic plants. This has been a source of controversy in landscape circles ever since the elder Olmsted* began the rescue of native species from the obscurity of local wild nature in the eastern U. S. The two extremes in this controversy have been approximately as follows: "A" rejects all local or regional wild plants as "weeds," common, vulgar, coarse, and so on; clears the land (perhaps a hangover from colonial days); and brings in refined garden species without reference to their original homeland. "B," on the other hand, rises in righteous indignation to the defense of the beauties of the local landscape and vegetation; condemns foreign introductions as disruptive of the local loveliness, inappropri-

* Olmsted, Frederick Law (1822–1903). Landscape architect best known for the design (with Calvert Vaux) of Central Park. Created countless other parks and private gardens. See page 20 for an essay by Olmsted.—Ed.

ate, blatant, gaudy, gauche, and so on, and as sickly exotics which will never be really healthy no matter how carefully pampered; whereas the lusty natives will grow and thrive with little or no care. This is another either/or controversy in which both sides have elements of both reason and prejudice. Here again the solution to the controversy lies in the selection and merging of the elements of reason, and the elimination of the elements of prejudice, from each side.

The range of plants useful to general landscape design extends from those surviving with reasonable health the normal local conditions—humanized-natural—through those surviving the local wild conditions. This entire range may include plants of both local and foreign origin. The variation in the proportioning of the two from the humanized to the wild habitat will depend on the degree of modification man finds necessary in the local climate and soil. Thus in a semi-arid climate like California the limiting factor on the use of native shrubs and trees in ordinary garden or park space is the amount of summer watering they will survive, in spite of their adaptation to summer-dryness. Certain technical problems of propagation and nursery handling also affect their availability and use. In the negative ecological zones the proportions of indigenous and introduced plants will vary considerably as we go from areas of intensive human cultural modification to wild areas; in the positive zones these proportions need not change greatly.

We come down, then, to specific problems of selecting the plant which will grow best while doing what we want it to do in a specific planned location. This selection will be based on our best analysis of soil and microclimate in that location, and our best prediction as to the future continuity of those conditions. Such selections should be made from the broadest possible list of available material. Restriction of the choice list is apt to eliminate the most relevant plant for a particular spot. The original nativity of the plants on the list is only relevant insofar as it may give us a clue to their adaptability to local conditions.

The esthetic aspects of the relation between native and foreign plants are more complex because more subjective. We must not fall into the trap of considering the local landscape we want to express as limited to that which existed before the white man came. The regional culture which exists at any given place and time is, as the geographers and planners point out, a complex of wild and humanized factors, and it is the humanizing which makes it a culture. At any specific given time—as 1950—when some of us decide to sit down to reconsider the situation in landscape design, we must consider the landscape we are living in, with its plant ecology—urban, rural, primeval—as a completed unit, a *fait accompli*, the site and the framework within which we must work. The past is history. We can learn from it, but no amount of nostalgia will bring it back.

In California today the landscape between urban and primeval is dominated more or less equally by the ragged verticality of the eucalyptus, a rankly persistent foreigner, and the sturdy horizontality of the live oak, an equally persistent native. These two forms help each other greatly by contrast in the landscape. Either dominant without the other would tend toward monotony of a thin or heavy cast. As a further example, we have four trees similar in use in the landscape: the live oak, a native; the olive, carob, and camphor, all exotics. The oak and the carob are similar in color, texture, and form; the carob is more limited by coolness. Olive and camphor are similar to the others in general form, but vary in color and texture: the one a billowy gray, the other a dappled light green. Their tolerance of heat and frost, hence their range, is somewhat greater than the others combined. The four together are rich and integral parts of the southwest tree culture; their origins are of only academic interest, except that they constitute a symbolic bridge from the old world of central and west Asia and the Mediterranean to the new world southwest.

ARRANGEMENT

Selection and arrangement have, of course, a mutually retroactive relation in the determination of the final planting. Selection of plants may be made to carry out the general space-form concepts of a freely-conceived plan, or a plan arrangement may be made to accommodate specific plants or plant interests demanded in the program. Parallel emphasis on space and materials as being of equal importance to the highest development of landscape design insures the possibility of fine work from either beginning. However the problem is approached, programmed, and developed, at some point someone has to make a specific decision as to the exact placement of each and every plant, and as to the selection of the kind of plant for each and every location. No amount of naturalizing, informality, good fellowship, or soft-pencil scribbling can evade this necessity. Each plant has a specific relation to every other plant in the vicinity. If this relation is not carefully considered and directed at some time before the plants are actually put in the ground, it becomes merely haphazard.

The concept of plant form as inseparable from space form, of the two as mutually dependent factors which, in combination, produce something richer than their mere addition, will eliminate much of the clumsiness, redundance, and heaviness of traditional kinds of planting, and still allow proper expression to the romantic search for pictorial and decorative quality. It will reduce the total quantity of plants used, give each plant proportionately more importance and character, increase the amount and feeling of space, and give it a clarity of form and richness of expression seldom achieved out-of-doors. It will tend to increase the direct relation between people and plants, i.e., make it possible for people to establish more or less direct contact with each of the larger plants, rather than to bury many of them in "mass planting."

Even though plants do have a structural use in the sense of giving form to space, their use is governed by few such laws or problems as those which force the fabrication of a building as one continuous shell or framework. Plants don't have to hold each other up. The relations established between these plant units, the ground, and structural elements depend entirely upon the plan-and-space concept of the designer. The plants can be spaced so far apart as never to touch, always to remain detached circles. Or they can be so crowded as to form continuous mats on the ground (lawns), masses above ground (screens), or canopies overhead (woods). They can be spaced regularly and geometrically, or completely irregularly, or any variation or combination between. Combinations of definite geometric plan skeletons with irregular clumps and groupings are both possible and desirable. Anything goes in plant grouping and arrangement if the people who are to see it like it, if it will grow well, and if the maintenance required is consistent with the nature of the plants and job program.

Arrangement of planting on most sites will proceed through the basic stages of surfacing, enclosure, shelter, and enrichment. These are the most practical stages, in terms of erosion control, screening, shade, and color. They are also the most esthetic stages in terms of the development of rich site-space form through the structural yet spatial use of plant material. In other words, we don't solve the practical prob-

lems first and then beautify them; we develop beautiful so-
lutions for the practical problems in their broadest definition,
which includes the human values needed in the landscape.

SURFACING

Organic surfacing is planting, commonly known as ground
cover. This is essentially plants set so close together that the
ground can't be seen from above, and, more important, the
rain cannot hit it directly. There are four general types of
planted surfacing: grass, or grass substitutes, which will take
traffic and mowing; spreading trees, so spaced as to form
complete coverage above the surface of the ground, and thus
control volunteer growth and erosion without blocking traffic; ground cover, which will not take traffic, or will obstruct
traffic (mat-formers, trailers, horizontal shrubs of any
height); and cultivation, the continuous maintenance of specific areas of bare ground around selected and more or less
changing flowers, vegetables, crops, or special shrubs or
trees. These are all cheaper to install than hard paving or
most inorganic surfacing, but most require maintenance
which eventually adds up to offset the saving in installation.

Grass in small areas makes special surfaces to sit or lie
on, specially shaped carpets or patterns of green, which also
reduce heat, glare, dust, noise. In large areas, such as parks
and general public grounds, grass is the most pleasant and
easily maintained ground surface control, establishing spacious continuity of surface (the meadow) and symbolic or
ideological continuity with the grasses which are the primary
control of the land surface of the earth. Use of grass beyond
these primary kinds of areas, as on steep banks or extended
tortuous strips and bays useless for sitting or pattern, tends
to be an irrational and wasteful use of material.

There is a considerable range in the finesse or refinement in treatment of grass areas, from the roughness of the natural wild meadow to the cultural precision of the bent-grass putting or bowling green. The ornamental counterpart of the latter, the *tapis vert,* the smooth lawn of one kind of grass, maintained by meticulous weeding, watering, fertilizing, mowing, and edging, is held up to us as the ideal, the peak objective for all grass-covered areas to aspire to. While this exact green carpet has its place, we are inclined to think it is a little mechanical in general application. Various mixes, of blue-grass and bent-grass and fine fescues, plus nurse crops and clover and daisies, seem to us to offer a richer palette for the grass area than the pure and unadulterated stand. They are, moreover, closer to a microcosm of the natural meadow, a more informal and easygoing surface. We have seen, in garden magazines, advocates of much more careful and complex miniatures of meadows, alpine and otherwise.

It has been said that a weed is merely a plant in the wrong place. Certainly in grass areas those invaders which grow in rosettes which destroy the continuity of the surface—as dandelions and plantains—or which freeze out and leave large bare patches in the lawns are definitely in the wrong place. But many mat-forming weeds in lawns—oxalis, chickweed, achillea—develop surfaces as pleasant as the grass itself. Dichondra, now popular as a grass substitute in the southwest, was once merely a "weed." The general idea of exploring the kinds of plants which will adapt themselves to the special conditions of traffic, mowing (however high), and constant sprinkling in most lawn areas, seems to us most pregnant. The surface must be smooth enough and resistant enough for comfortable walking, it must maintain a fairly constant color and texture; within those limits there should be considerable room for experiment.

Mat, trailing, and shrub covers are useful on areas which

will not be used for living purposes because of slope, bad location, or in some cases a surplus of land. Thus, fill and soft cut banks, or probably any slope greater than fifteen percent, are most practically planted with such covers. They are apt to be more interesting in color and texture, and more tenacious and persistently green with less maintenance, than grasses for slope control. Particularly as the slopes become dry, sterile, or rocky, these mat, trailing, and shrub covers become more reliable. Around buildings they also reduce heat, dust, noise, and glare.

Beyond such practical considerations ground-cover plants constitute a design element of considerable importance. The larger kinds of shrubs which grow up to or above eye level, become also enclosure elements, obstructing or baffling vision as well as movement. Below eye level there is still a considerable variation in heights, say from three inches up to four feet, within which very rich and interesting junior spatial relations in form, color, and texture are possible. Here we begin to overlap the herbaceous border. The distinction between the two is simply that ground-cover planting is relatively permanent, herbaceous border planting relatively impermanent. The two can, of course, work together. Ground-cover plants, in the mat, trailer, and spreading shrub forms, run the gamut of textures from fine to coarse, and have also a considerable range in color of foliage, flower, and fruit, particularly in the milder regions. In addition to the more obvious examples these forms include such hardy elements as bulbs and tubers—day-lily and iris—and many succulents and cacti in the southwest. Thus, building on the French parterre, Victorian carpet bedding, modern German and Swiss alpine gardens, and the English color border, even as Burle Marx, we have broad opportunities for design in free modern three-dimensional patterns, below eye level where they can be understood. The ground-cover area is somewhat comparable to water in spatial terms, in that it tends to block physical but not visual movement. Bearing in mind the primary relation of people by quantity to space for living by square footage and cubage, such patterns can become rich contexts, surrounds, borders, and inserts in the general usable surfacing of grass and paving. Where, to conserve water or labor, grass is eliminated, paving, ground cover, and trees can be expanded and related in new proportions and patterns of shade, greenery, color, and spacious surface.

ENCLOSURE

As we move to the consideration of plant forms relevant to the enclosure of garden space at the sides, we move toward plants of more erect growth, whose vertical dimension tends to exceed their horizontal; whereas in ground-cover plants the horizontal tends to exceed the vertical. There are, of course, certain radical clump forms which fall between and can be used for either. Enclosure plants will have, in general, an equal or superior relation to the eye-level plane, that is, from five feet up. Their height, density, and evergreenness will be gauged by the need for screening, privacy, and protection from intrusion by life or wind. At a certain point in intensity of land use—as, probably, the fifty-foot or smaller backyard—planted screens become ineffective or unreliable as guarantors of privacy or controllers of movement. At this point structural control becomes functionally relevant, because reliable.

Within such conditions it will be seen that the range of choice in form, texture, and color is as broad as the available range of larger herbs, grasses, and shrubs, of trees, and of vines supported structurally. All the shrubbery border material—facer, filler, background—the hedge material, the smaller trees, the vines, the larger odds and ends that have been consigned to the wild garden, the cactus garden, the tropical or desert garden, or some other pigeon-hole, take on new vitality, new interest, new richness, when we consider them thoroughly and creatively in relation to this concept of enclosure, of qualitative space formation.

When we combine this variety at expanded outdoor scale with the space-form concepts of modern art and architecture, based as they are at their best on careful distillation of the primary space-form relations of our world, new vistas and potentialities for beauty in the landscape open up before us. The free and creative organization of planes, masses, and structural patterns in space above the ground plane, as an abstract or diagrammatic basis for the development of actual practical plant and structure relations on the site, will exceed in the beauty and variety of its production any mechanically haphazard (informal) or haphazardly mechanical (formal) academic system now in use. The gamut of three-dimensional relations—rectangular, angular, circular, or more complex—is richer than any sterile axes, any "informal" sprinkling or squiggling, that has been offered to date.

As the demands of screening, privacy, and protection decrease, our range in choice of enclosure material will expand. The solid plant screen gives us primarily variations in color and texture of foliage. As its necessity for solidity recedes—as it becomes, perhaps, more playful or fantastic space elaboration within a general enclosure—variations in structural pattern, in relation of foliage to ground, and in fruit and flower color become part of the spatial palette.

SHELTER

The line between trees and shrubs is arbitrary, and there are many kinds which overlap it under varying conditions of growth. If we say that a tree is a plant which gets up high enough and spreads its branches widely enough for us to walk under them, we will find that there are single-trunked forms (as small flowering fruits or dwarf maples) which are not tall enough, or (as Lombardy poplars or Italian cypresses) broad enough to qualify. On the other hand there are many-stemmed forms—carobs, olives, privets, crepe myrtle—which do. Many of these can be either shrub or tree form, depending on soil, moisture, pruning, and so on. There are many good small tree or semi-tree forms which are commonly forced into the role of shrubs, with inevitable distortions from crowding and trimming. Likewise there are good large shrub forms which are often distorted by training into unhappy imitations of trees. Such distinctions come down to specific decisions with specific plants and cultural practices. Woody plants develop through juvenile, mature, and aged forms, and many of them may pass from shrub to tree form after the first or second of these. Thus the relation between shrub and tree forms is not really as simple as the nursery catalogues. It is a question of spacing, based on understanding of the relation between ultimate size and rate of growth of the specific plant, and of the distinction between trimming and pruning. . . .

Definition of tree forms as those spreading foliage over our heads is a result of the classification of plants in terms of space relations. Shrubs give enclosure at the *sides* of our garden or park spaces, to any height, and with any degree of thickness or thinness. Trees give additional enclosure, or *shelter,* overhead. This again varies through all the degrees of darkness, heaviness, lightness, and thinness, plus the seasonal alternations of deciduous forms, plus the variations in structure from simple radial symmetry to complex several-trunked irregularity, plus the richness of flower or fruit in many kinds.

There is a specific functional value in deciduous trees,

which we tend to ignore in our milder south and west zones in concentrating on evergreen material. This is the fact that they provide shade in the summer when it is needed, and let in the sun in winter when it is needed. This simple fact makes deciduous trees (sycamores, elms, maples) the most relevant large trees for use anywhere close to buildings (except perhaps on the north side) or over garden or park spaces which are to receive fairly intensive use. The space beneath the big evergreen tree, cool and breezy in the hot summer, becomes dank and forbidding during cold and wet winter months.

Further functional values are brought out by Fitch:

> Certain aspects of the landscape are susceptible to wide and flexible manipulation, the health and comfort potentials of which have been scarcely tapped by contemporary designers. Two illustrations will suffice: the use of trees and use of lawns in urban areas. Above and beyond their beauty, the scientific use of deciduous trees will accomplish any or all of the following:
>
> Deflect, absorb, and reduce the heat radiation. . . .
>
> Reduce the free air temperatures. . . .
>
> Filter the atmosphere. . . .
>
> Reduce intensities and glare. . . .
>
> Increase visual privacy. . . .
>
> Reduce the transmission of airborne sound. . . .
>
> In general, trees have a stabilizing effect upon their immediate surroundings, reducing all environmental extremes. Rudolph Geiger, in his excellent study on the micro-climate, found that a mixed for-

est growth of spruce, oak, and poplar cuts off sixty-nine percent of the sun's heat from the ground. He found that forests are cooler in summer, warmer in winter than clear land; and that a belt of trees would reduce wind velocities by as much as sixty-three percent. . . .

Certainly trees have been the friends of man ever since he first settled down on the land, providing him with shade and greenery, color and shelter, fruit and timber, and improving the local soil and climate in the process. We can scarcely improve on the many rich words which have been spoken and written in appreciation of trees. Our definition of them as elements both in space and enclosing space may seem somewhat arty or intellectual, but it will add a new dimension and a new coherence to their use in the landscape. At the scale of park, neighborhood, and community, trees become potentially the primary integrating and co-ordinating pattern, linking together buildings, roads and open space—architecture, engineering, and landscape—into a continuity of space pattern and ground organization impossible without them. This potential is seldom seen in actuality in our urban landscapes, but it is present in any well-developed rural landscape.

Many planners and architects feel that it is necessary or desirable to bring about and preserve a contrasting separation between town and country "to prevent the drowning of both in suburbia." In England Sharp, Colvin, and others have sought to achieve this separation by architectural integration of dwellings into multi-family or row houses, whose larger masses contrast sharply with the countryside and tend to emphasize the relative concentration of towns. This idea, however, is in conflict with the great American dream of a detached house for each family on an ample plot of ground. It is noteworthy that trees in organized patterns (not necessarily regular or geometric) furnish a way to resolve the contradiction. Used thus, they can pull together and give unity to the heterogeneous collection of single-family detached houses that make up our American neighborhoods, welding them into coherently integrated communities that stand out distinctly against the adjacent open lands.

The tall trees—poplars and elms and pines, eucalyptus and palms, cedar and cypress—make the major spatial backbone, the uplifting skeleton of our general tree patterns. The spreading, irregular or round-headed forms—oak and mulberry, camphor and olive, rubber and fig—make the secondary horizontal shelter or overhead enclosure pattern. The small trees—flowering fruits and citrus, birches and small palms and tall shrubs—make a third intimate detailed partial-enclosure pattern, the fanciful counterpoint, the final color and interest and richness. Trees, along with structures and vehicles, are the basic tools for establishing secure and stable scale relations between people and landscapes large or small, serene or picturesque. They provide measures with which the individual can determine sizes and distances, and thereby establish his relationship to the world around him.

Finally, we must reject that most childish of naïvetés: that the symmetrical tree with the prominent leader should be used "formally" (regularly), and the more irregular tree "informally" (irregularly). This is the kind of oversimplification which stops all design processes before they have fairly begun. We must contrast with this dictum the proposition that the most regular trees should be placed most irregularly on the ground, the most irregular in quite regular arrangements, and then go on from there to the real rich complexities of spatial planting design.

The anarchy of tree pattern in our towns and cities is an expression of an anarchy of land use which is becoming socially wasteful and therefore obsolete. Control of street tree patterns within public rights-of-way is a beginning but merely accentuates the anarchy within the blocks. Truly democratic organization of our general community tree patterns, block by block and neighborhood by neighborhood, can be projected for an expanding future. Current spots of mechanical irregularity in parks, and of the sterile formality of authority, will be swallowed up in this tremendous tree symphony of the future. Designers of planting for housing projects and planned communities who have taken the easy way of the haphazard sprinkling of trees throughout the site have undoubtedly missed a golden opportunity to project such great patterns as these.

In ecological terms, the climax vegetation most suited to man's habitat is a varying combination of forest and savannah (tree-sprinkled grassland). As human sociology (ecology) moves toward the delicate and harmonious balance-in-motion of plant and animal ecology, the vegetative pattern of the urban environment will tend to lose its disorder, its distortion of material, its haphazard anarchy, and move likewise toward the coherence, the clarity, and the strength of the primeval and rural patterns. As this happens the rural pattern, too, will grow richer and stronger. In due time, as democratic processes achieve constantly greater portions of their potential for human welfare, and develop expanding stability and cultural expression in the landscape, the present scale of landscape values will tend to reverse itself. Instead of moving from the ugly city toward the peak of wilderness beauty, it will be possible to move from the wilderness, through constantly more magnificent and orderly rural refinements of the face of the earth, to urban communities composed of structures, paving, grass, shrubs and trees, which are rich, sparkling, crystalline nuclei in the web of spatial relations that surrounds the earth—peak expressions of the reintegration of man and nature; the final conservation of the earth's resources.

The Forest is a corporation of many kinds of plants.
The most conspicuous are trees, . . . The Forest is
an organism always in motion with all its parts in-
terrelated and acting on each other. These parts are
dense thickets; warm, dry, open hillsides; lakes and
streams; bogs and bottomlands; open glades with
carpets of wild flowers; moist, cool ravines deep in
ferns—all are within the Forest.

PLATT

Even so, the humanized savannah-forest climax will be rich,
varied, complex, yet orderly; including the dwellings, the
workspaces, and the recreation spaces, indoors and out, of a
healthy democratic population. Even so, the magnificent concepts of community pattern will not forget, but rather will be
based on, the relation of man, woman, and child to tree,
bush, flower bed, and grass plot. The scale relation between
open space and the enclosing or organizing elements—the
horizontal and the vertical—will be primary. The latter must
not encroach on the former to the point of claustrophobia,
nor the former on the latter to the point of agoraphobia. In
the negative ecological sections we push and promote post-
climax tree growth out from organized centers in orderly
patterns; in the positive zones we push the subclimax grassland and more refined open spaces out against and into the
resurgent forest blanket.

Surfacing, enclosure, and shelter are the primary elements of the garden, the park, or the humanized landscape,
even as they are of our more refined structural habitations
and workplaces. These establish the primary form, character, and space relations of the outdoor space. If they are
conceived with imagination and sensitivity the space will be
beautiful and satisfying with no more material added. If they

are conceived in haste and "practicality," or in the sterile blindness of the academic approach, they will be lucky to become pleasing by the grace of the growth of the plants in them. Otherwise all the "beautification," the flower borders and foundation plants in the world will not save them from dullness.

MARIAN CRUGER COFFIN
(1876–1957)

*Marian Coffin designed gardens with an effect of delicate
naturalism. Her planting designs were essays in superb form
and texture, appropriately highlighted with sculptural shrubs
and small trees, which vividly accented the important parts
of the composition. I have had the opportunity to view some
of the gardens that still exist, and her wise planting choices
have come into their maturity with great distinction. Her
overall designs are sensitive yet quite fragile, and age has
worn many of them down; however, they are excellent
candidates for skillful restoration.*

TREES AND SHRUBS
FOR LANDSCAPE EFFECTS

Green and Other Gardens

There are good opportunities for arranging some special type of garden in connection with a woodland setting, if not actually in the woods themselves. One color note that always seems difficult to place properly in the average garden, or in groupings on the lawn where it is apt to clash with reds, oranges, salmons, and strong yellows, is amaranth, be it the true form or one of the paler tints that lead up to vibrant magenta. These tones never seem at their best when in sunshine or when seen on all sides in the open, as they require a certain amount of shadow and mystery to bring out their really lovely and elusive qualities. Well placed this color can be a gardening triumph, badly placed a catastrophe.

Why not horrify your friends and create a landscape picture that any artist will applaud by making a magenta garden? The place for such a garden is in connection with woods, if possible; or, at least off by itself and well shadowed by trees. We have one small or medium-growing tree that is invaluable for the height and proper color for our composition—the native Judas tree, or Redbud (Cercis canadensis). Its cousin, the more compact Chinese variety (Cercis chinensis) will also contribute the same quality. The bloom to me is one of the most exquisite things in nature and the contrast of the tiny, rosy purple flowers with the dark bark of the branches before the leaves appear in spring is unlike any

Source: New York: Charles Scribner's Sons, 1940.

be appropriate to use in connection with an important house. Boxwood, of course, would be the first choice (where it is hardy or where it can be protected in winter), and will make a garden alone. We have the different forms from which to choose. The tall true Tree Box (Buxus sempervirens arborescens), with its graceful growth and feathery foliage—a plant or two of this will be essential to have in the background to give variety and height. It is difficult to obtain from the nurseries in any large size, but if one is in luck a tree of some age may be met with, growing near an old farmhouse, from New Jersey south, and can be moved in by competent people. Then, for medium size, the more usual Buxus sempervirens and its various forms and shapes. For the foreground and main effects the incomparable English Box (B. sempervirens suffruticosa), used in different sizes. These types will make an all Boxwood garden that will always be handsome, distinguished, and dignified. Its plan may be an irregular grouping about a grass center, fairly wide and open, or the center may be further marked by a quiet pool reflecting the changing, passing shadows of the day. Or again the grass may be reduced or omitted, with a stylized design of intricate pattern in its place, which with a little more elaboration could be developed into the form of a maze.

A fine Box planting could have the addition of a few unusual evergreens, such as a tree or two of Holly or of the strong-growing evergreen Privet, Ligustrum lucidum, or of Viburnum rhytidophyllum. Also a few flowering trees of distinct sculptural quality would be in order, such as the Magnolias. Here too would be the opportunity to use an accent of the choice Gordonia or of Stewartia pentagyna, its lovely summer-blooming relative, hardy but for some reason neglected and difficult to obtain.

Such a garden can be made with safety only from Philadelphia south, unless one is happy having a specially shel-

other tree or shrub. They will stand a certain amount of shade and so can be planted in an open clearing in the wood, or on its edge, where they will be a contrast to the background of the taller forest growers, in delicate froth of opening leaves and buds in palest chartreuse green, and yellow.

Though maroon rather than magenta, Magnolia lenni is another medium-size tree to employ if your arrangement is apart—more in the open—as it is not appropriate for woodland planting. The great flowers, borne before the leaves, have a splendid depth, and make, as all the dark colors do, a foil for the more brilliant shades. The smaller, more bushlike M. nigra is less spreading, more uncommon, and contributes the same color in dark maroon bloom.

For the midrib of the picture it will be possible to use all sorts of Azaleas that are of this color range, A. amœna in pure magenta and some of the hybrids in bright pink hues of a bluish cast, like A. hinodegiri and A. hinomayo, and the rosy purple A. macrantha and the lower kurumes in brilliant carmine pinks, making the entire planting complete in itself.

Or a bolder effect may be made by omitting the smaller kurumes and retaining only a few of the larger Azaleas, using for the main planting the stronger types of the hybrid Rhododendrons and some of the true dwarf species like R. wilsoni, R. punctatum, and R. myrtifolium to bring the taller plants down to the edge. The hybrid Rhododendrons are usually in tones of blue pinks, carmines, and crimsons that lead up well to, and will harmonize with, the true magenta of Azalea amœna, though a few are a dull unattractive amaranth.

Almost all these hybrids are exceedingly handsome for foliage plants as well as for bloom. The magenta note is perhaps best represented by Caractacus, Parson's grandiflora, and van der Hoopen on the red side, with Kettledrum verging toward a dark crimson, and with purpureum grandiflorum and purpureum elegans in more purple tones, as their names imply. It would be quite possible to use these in separate groups, or to allow them to mingle in a fuchsia-like blend which could be further emphasized by some dashing pinks like Henrietta Sargent and Mrs. C. S. Sargent, or by the rose crimson of Abraham Lincoln. Our native Rhododendrons are invaluable plants for woodland conditions, for using in really deep shade (a location not so acceptable to the hybrids), and for forming tall, dense backgrounds for the choicer varieties. The Great Laurel (Rosebay) R. maximum is hardy far north and has pale mauve-pink flowers. R. catawbiense is the more southern representative, but hardy as far as New England; both bloom from June into July, but the leaves of the latter are less long and shiny, more rounded, and the flowers a dull amaranth tone.

As Azaleas and Rhododendrons are fairly expensive plants, for our woodland magenta garden we can replace them with herbaceous material, always provided that the glade is open enough and that the ground has been freed from too many hungry tree roots. Still retain the Judas tree for the chief glory in spring, and with it use quantities of dwarf Phlox, Iris pumila in buff yellow and maroon, Silenes, Bleeding Hearts and the magenta tree Peony (P. moutan), the type. The Japanese Primroses (Primula sieboldi) and their hybrids are about eighteen inches high and will vary the tonality, as will the whites, creams, and pale yellows of the dwarfer and exquisite Munstead strain. Straw-colored daffodils can run in and out between the shrubs, and the early Iris pumila, Marocain, a deep maroon, will further accent the edge. Later on, as these things fade, large drifts of pink Foxgloves, the more unusual buff variety (Digitalis ambigua) and the German Iris, Kochi, a deep-purple, blooming with them or a little before, will give just the fillip needed; then if you wish to continue the magenta pictures in your wood all

through the summer, Joe-Pye-Weed and Loosestrife and others of our wild flowers will be very telling, as well as the Beauty Berry (Callicarpa japonica) for its unusual jewel-like purple fruit.

The combinations and variations on these themes are endless, as one could run the color gamut from palest blush pink on up through strong blue-pinks into real magenta, and so to a wine-red maroon. For associates and contrasts creamy whites and very pale yellows are capital; gray foliage is an important asset, as the silvery tones are an admirable foil to the stronger color. Blues are seldom good, as they lower the key of the scheme too much, sadden it, or muddy it. Strong oranges, yellows, and salmons are discordant; so, too, is very bright red; but just a touch of scarlet will key up the whole composition, though care must be exercised that only a very little is used.

From the strident tones of magenta, which are better taken in small doses, we can turn to the restfulness of green plantings. By using only woody plants for foliage effects one can achieve a most satisfying type of garden, to be enjoyed all the year round. It will be a fine deep-green note of a certain solidarity in spring, when all flowering plants are budding and bursting; in summer a relief from almost too much warmth and color; in autumn again a setting for the flaming falling leaves, later retaining its beauty in contrast to the bare winter branches and snowy landscape. A green garden can be equally successful in sunlight or in shadow; in a formal design or in an informal one; near the house or far from it. For its component elements it may be made of the most expensive evergreens, or of evergreens of less costly varieties, or, when seen only in summer, of deciduous trees and shrubs of good foliage, or of a combination of both.

Let us first consider the best type of material that would

tered spot on Long Island or in New Jersey. Not that Box cannot be planted with a good chance of surviving winters farther north, as can easily be proved by the many fine old pieces, as well as hedges, of Box that lived after the severe winters of 1933–1934 and 1935, even in New England—but one cannot be sure. However, if expense and labor are not deterrents, the dwarfer forms can be protected in winter and you can have your Box Garden with comparative safety as far north as Rhode Island. The low, soft, spreading Buxus microphylla and its variety koreana, having a distinct habit of growth, are said to be hardy as far north as Boston, and in my experience it has been so in Connecticut. They should become a valuable addition to our evergreens, when there are not enough plants available to supply a demand.

As I have said before, the handsome and hardy Yew may well be called the Boxwood of New England, and every year is becoming more known and more appreciated. Suppose we wish to make a Green Garden where it is not possible to use Box; substitute Yew in its various forms and the result will be fine, less expensive, and the plants will withstand severe climatic conditions.

If a tallish stiff hedge is required, Taxus media hicksii [sic] and Taxus cuspidata capitata are the thing. For less stiff and broader effects, Taxus media and the true Taxus cuspidata as well as many of its forms are good for midrib planting. Taxus canadensis is very low and spready, and Taxus repandens is noteworthy for its graceful drooping habit. For dwarf hedges, particularly valuable in gardens is the slow-growing Box-like Taxus brevifolia, and for very small hedges, that can really be kept in bounds as the edging of a flower bed, Taxus canadensis stricta is invaluable. This is a great advantage, as most Yews are such strong growers that they must have room to spread out and it is difficult to restrain them in a small compass.

197

A Yew Garden, like a Box Garden, with some accents of flowering trees, would be entirely complete and handsome as a unit in itself, or other evergreens could be introduced. For such an association the spiny small-leafed Barberries, all with yellow flowers and dull-bloomed black fruit, would be an interesting contrast, as would the Firethorn (Pyracantha coccinea lalandi), with glossier foliage and most decorative orange berries. Berberis julianæ and Berberis sargentiana are upright, branching, and medium-size; Berberis gagnepaini is more compact. Berberis triacanthophora grows only about three to five feet high and equally wide, is a distinct plant, and for this reason makes a good accent. With them try some small trees, interesting not only for bloom but also for berries. There are two hardy plants of this type that one seldom sees—the mountain Ash and the Turquoise Berry (Symplocos paniculata). Though the Mountain Ash is always a favorite where it is known, few people know the Symplocos, which is a nicely shaped shrub or small tree, well proportioned enough to use as a specimen on a lawn, and has a pretty inflorescence; but its unique glory is the real turquoise-blue fruit, borne in profusion in autumn, not showy from a distance but lovely close at hand.

For use either with Box or Yew, or for complete groupings by themselves, is that array of broad-leaved evergreens, the Rhododendron hybrids, the Kalmias, the Andromedas and the less hardy kurume and Indian Azaleas. These are glossier of foliage than the Barberries, more elegant and handsomer in appearance, and, of course, have the most beautiful and showy flowers of all. So why not try a garden of these alone, using only such varieties as have white or palest blush-pink flowers; making it at a distance from the house and leading the way to it through some specially designed *allée*? It would at all seasons be a retreat from the world, restful in its beauty, and when in bloom one of the greatest delights of the gardening year. For accent trees try, if the scheme be not too formal, an old Apple or two, or some of the spreading Crabs, such as Malus scheideckeri, or, for more formal use, white or pink English Hawthorns. The Cornels fall imperceptibly into this picture, our unsurpassable white Dogwood (Cornus florida) and the more formal pink (Cornus florida rubra), as would the other tree of the family, the alternate-leaved Cornel (C. alternifolia), whose snowy flowers come after the leaves have developed.

For very informal plantings, in contrast to these rather elaborate effects, a green garden can be equally charming worked out with some of the simpler native things that are evergreen, or those that keep a deep green all summer, though they may be deciduous. It would be rather an advantage if it were placed at some distance from the house—a spot to wander to and discover by means of a winding path—though it could be readily adapted to serve the purpose of an outdoor living room in connection with a simple country place or a cottage by the sea.

For a planting entirely of evergreens we could use an all-Juniper effect; these, being native, or in harmony with natives, would be most appropriate, and are of course easy to grow and are hardy. Choose Cedars (J. virginiana) in varying heights for the tall spiky effects, our Savin [sic] (J. sabina) and its variety J. tamariscifolia for medium wide growth, and the innumerable varieties of low, spreading, and prostrate forms to bring the others down to the front.

If more contrast is wanted, add Locusts for their scent and charming white bloom, some Sassafras and Sweet Gum (Liquidambar) trees to give form and autumn color, as well as the native Hawthorns. The Cockspur Thorn (Cratægus crus-galli) is a plant of much character, so thorny and intricately branched that it is the bane of gardeners at planting time. The Washington Thorn (C. cordata) is taller, more symmetrical, and it, like innumerable other varieties of our indigenous species, has fine white flower bracts, showy red to orange fruit, and a generally branching habit. For a ground cover with these the evergreen Bearberry (Arctostaphylos uva-ursi) would be a capital plant for use with the Junipers, and nothing could be better to clothe a dry bank. Such a planting would be adapted to a sandy hilly situation.

There is another group of plants which (though deciduous) keep the deep color of their leaves so well all summer that they are a valuable substitute at that season for the evergreens. These are the Bayberries, Sweet Ferns, Blueberries, our native Azalea arborescens, tall-growing, with fragrant flowers in late May or June, and, naturally associating with these, the equally fragrant Sweet Pepper Bush (Clethra alnifolia). As these are lovers of peat-soil, humus, and low ground we could introduce all sorts of unusual carpeting things that require such conditions, to cover the spaces between them.

There is that interesting group of low, creeping native plants for which it is so difficult to find the proper home—the Box Huckleberry (Gaylussacia brachycera); a very rare plant, the Cowberry (Vaccinium vitis-idæa), forming dense broad mats two inches high; the better-known Wintergreen (Gaultheria procumbens; the Partridgeberry (Mitchella repens), with its gay red berries; and the tiny white-flowered shrub, Pachistima [*Paxistima*] canbyi, can all be tried if you will take special pains with their cultivation.

Other delightful plants for country surroundings, either in low situations or equally at home on drier land, would be our tall deciduous Holly (Ilex verticillata), sometimes called Black Alder—a poor name as it is not an Alder and is not black. As, like all its family, it is a diœcious plant, both male and female individuals must be planted to insure the attractive, long-retained red berries. The Inkberry, our other native, is evergreen, and would add its glossy foliage and black fruit to this picture, as would the Fothergillas, in spring almost as showy as the Dogwoods, and like them changing in autumn into flaming colors. Though perfectly hardy at least to New England, they are practically unknown and unplanted. For more treelike growth we could again use the Sweet Gum, the Tupelo, and the charming Magnolia glauca, with its shyly borne blooms often continuing until frost and succeeded by handsome fruit.

THOMAS DOLLIVER CHURCH
(1902–1978)

Thomas Church achieved an international reputation and is undoubtedly the best-known American landscape architect since Frederick Law Olmsted. He was able to make the transition between the beaux-arts garden (which he studied at Harvard's Graduate School of Design) and that of the modern Californian garden (which he created). His designs are timeless and practical. They are based on the intelligent development of the unique site in conjunction with an understanding of the special needs of the owner. He listened to his clients carefully, and then provided for them with inspiration.

———————

GARDENS ARE FOR PEOPLE
HOW TO PLAN FOR OUTDOOR LIVING

Good Property Is No Longer Easy to Find

The perfect site is on a slightly rising ground with large healthy trees, a fine view, or a beautiful background of foliage; it has deep, rich topsoil and is oriented to be out of the wind—but to catch all the sunshine. As long as we're dreaming, we might as well add that it is near schools, churches, and shops and that all utilities are already at the property line. If you find it, buy it.

If you're going to look for property, take your architect and landscape architect along—they are qualified to advise you. The real estate agent is not trained to tell you if it's a suitable site for you. His business is to sell it. The landscape architect can measure your requirements and your budget against the probable cost of developing the property. Maybe the trees are either poor varieties or in bad condition; maybe it's covered with obnoxious weeds which would be almost impossible to eradicate. There may be grading problems that aren't obvious. There may be indications of poor drainage, heavy clay soil, erosion, or exposure that should influence your decision. If you're looking at the property on a hot summer day and find it lush and cool, you may forget it's a north slope with no sun from October to March.

Most people start out with a budget. The only way to hope to stay within it is to avoid as much guesswork as you can and to

Source: New York: Reinhold Publishing Corporation, 1955.

know all possible costs before you commit yourself. To the average layman the headings are simple: the lot, the house, the furniture, the garden (it will be done gradually later). The garden allowance covers only soil preparation, plants, and lawns.

But—*ever hear of site improvements?* They're seldom included in the first budget and yet they are real costs. Aside from special conditions imposed by the site or the client's whims they consist of tree clearing and rough grading, boundary fences, entrance road and parking, additional leveling and fine grading after the house is built, retaining walls, drainage system, hose bibs and sprinklers, garden structure (tool house, bath house, extra storage), screen fences within the garden and garden lighting. Most of them should be done before you move on. On a simple, flat lot they may not strain your budget, but on tough terrain they may cost as much as the house itself.

Don't cross your fingers and hope the bids will come low. They won't. The things you will have to eliminate may be the things you want most.

Find out where you're going before you start.

FLETCHER STEELE
(1885–1971)

Fletcher Steele's work, Gardens and People, *was published fourteen years after* Landscape for Living, *yet it seems dated. I think this is because of its essential conservatism. There is also a strong oriental influence in Steele's design work. This is reflected in the actual structural details of his gardens and in his choice of plantings. His remarks in "China Knows" form a philosophical basis for his very distinguished work.*

———————

GARDENS AND PEOPLE

China Knows

CHINA TEACHES THE LANDSCAPE ARCHITECT

"Too much emphasis on slopes and banks makes the work crude; too much emphasis on calm and quiet is trite; too much emphasis on humanity makes the work commonplace; too much emphasis on houses and arbors makes it confused; too much emphasis on stones makes it bony; while too much emphasis on soil makes it fleshy."

KUO HSI (SUN DYNASTY A.D. 960–1279)

. . .

CHINESE FRIENDS IN THE GARDEN

The Chinese avoids accumulation of objects in the garden until he is sure they are wanted and will be wanted for a long time. He does not like to be surprised either agreeably or otherwise. He is not interested for more than a minute in novelties. To be sure, he will fill his garden for an idle hour with dancing mice or trained bears; with infant sword dancers or a shadow play; perhaps with an arrangement of

Source: Boston: Houghton Mifflin Company (The Riverside Press Cambridge), 1964.

flowerpots. But he will not clutter it for a year with unfamiliar plant growth on the trivial hope roused by some tradesman's word that it will be pink and flower in August. He remembers that he does not always like pink flowers; and how will it look during the other months when it is not in bloom?

Formalities hold strangers in the outer courts. Plants, too, must go through a careful novitiate. They must be studied, and their habits and temper known. They must live and flower with virtue, and die suitably. For the death of a flower is watched with intent, poetic philosophy. Gardens, to the Chinese, represent life in all completeness, not the hour of rich fulfillment alone. They will have no plant that is not a friend, to be watched and tended as long as it lives, come good, come ill.

The Chinese would as easily say of his wife as of his garden: "You should have seen her last week when she was all dressed up." His pride in his wife and garden are too deep, too much part of his home, to wear on his sleeve, for visitors to peck at. When the precious moment comes, when the moon is right and the peach tree is coming into flower next the pond, he will invite a close friend to share his pleasure without distraction of yesterday or tomorrow. No man is invited casually to come any time and stay as long as he likes—nor is a plant.

BOUQUETS ON THE BRANCH

The Chinese make their bouquets on the branch. As the sun rises on the peonies in Peking Central Park, the maker of flower arrangements studies the plants for inspiration. An idea arrives. A plant is chosen. An opening blossom is pulled out and staked on slender bamboo. Yesterday's faded flower is retired. The weak stem of tomorrow's bud is wired. Inharmonious lines and masses are hidden away. What is too long is mysteriously shortened without being cut. What is too short is stretched and its position changed. The plant is made to look its best for a day. A common peony becomes a handsome flower arrangement.

The American at a flower show works furiously for a few weeks on "backgrounds" and "accessories" and concocts special gardens to glorify his plants. The Chinese spreads this energy over the year in his own garden. He puts an awning over a single flower to temper the heat at midday. When it looks tired, he spatters water, not for its roots but to cool its aching head. Jars and pots are brought in from time to time, not for the plants growing in them but to add contrasting form and color as suggested by the season.

The Chinese gardener deliberates on permanent arrangements of still life and growing plants to decorate his courtyards. Handsome stones are moved for hundreds of miles over terrible roads. With infinite thought and patience they are combined to make a picture, sometimes alone on the pavement, sometimes softened by a peony or two. Then for generations the peony is watched and trained to bring out beauty of stem, leaf and flower, always sparsely and economically. For temperate Chinese sentiment seems to regard opulent vegetation much as fastidious people at home feel about the Fat Lady in the circus.

While conventions are strong, there are no rigid rules in China. Flower arrangement is a matter of taste, and nobody judges it with a tape measure as is done in Japan. Moreover, all the proprieties in China are easy because they are a bit casual. Flower arrangements are well-groomed but never dressy.

The Chinese are whimsical and they must get many a chuckle, first and last, out of flower arrangement. They like unexpected and incongruous scale. Whether in lines or groups, things are often set in ludicrous juxtaposition. Tiny combinations of pebbles and moss grow out of a huge porcelain tub. A six-foot feather duster of a plant somehow balances in a diminutive pot. The details are always good-natured. Whatever they do, the whole effect is decorative and suitable. The Chinese is a professional artist at heart. His whole garden is more important than any single tree or flower or pond.

CHINESE HUMOR

The Presbyterian is not encouraged to laugh at serious matters and his straight jacket twitches in China. Chinese joy in the incongruous is overstrong, he uncomfortably feels, for nothing in religion, family piety or reverence for things seen or unseen lies altogether outside raillery. The American is not convinced that it evades impious ridicule when he sees hilarity at funerals. But the Chinese seem to respect the more those symbols of the universe at which, in good companionship, gods and men can smile together. The sound of the chuckle is over the land.

Gardens, naturally, do not escape. How the last old Empress must have giggled in the Summer Palace when building a marble boat with the millions borrowed from us to launch a navy! Even the dragons grin. Pagodas are buried in the desert where no man can see them, exquisitely carved and painted. A twelve-inch gutter is bridged with marble lace that belongs in a museum doll's house. A kingfisher's feather is framed with pearls.

Mummery it is, perhaps, and extravagant. It is cheerful, too. After all, is it less worthy than a solemn greenhouse of unceasingly expensive orchids that are gone in a night? Less useful than a race course? Is a precious work of art less suitable in a garden than over a mantel? Is it less important because it helps the world to smile?

YANG AND YIN

After struggling with the language for some months in China, the American comes away with two words, Yang and Yin. He remembers them because they have expanded his understanding of some simple facts.

In his native tongue he has used the nouns male and female with assurance. He could give some account of what he means by masculine, but has always shied away from the label "feminine," preferring to leave real battles to the ladies. "Why invite bedevilment? " he says. "Such matters play their part in life but none in philosophy." The poor ostrich!

The Chinese philosopher insists that nothing be excluded from his argument. Nevertheless, he too, dislikes suffering in the home and is wise. Ages ago he saw masculine and feminine adjectives sometimes refuse to stick to their nouns. For in China not all men are brave winners of bread, and some women won't stay put in the kitchen just to please the dictionary. So in his sensible way, the Oriental decided that it was not facts or adjectives but principles that counted. He called the male principle Yang and the female Yin, which words are short and easy to remember.

No sooner was this settled than he caught sight of Yang and Yin no matter where he looked, not least in landscapes and gardens. The earth, its inertia, its resistance to change, its hunger for life and disregard of life's surplus, wedded to eternal willingness to help, is Yin. Man's will to use the earth, to cultivate it, build on it, mine into it, subject it to his need and convenience, is Yang. Active and passive, what man wants and what must be, is the Chinese wedding of principles by which is begotten a balanced life.

A constant regard for compelling factors which cannot be obliterated but can be maneuvred somewhat by help of thought, time and labor actually control every gardener and every garden. But only in China are they welcomed in the program as partners of the designer. The good garden bears witness to balance of Yang and Yin.

The Chinese regard what we call "constructive" ideas and work as Yang. They are part of aspiration which is conceived as the vertical element in the visual world, the embodiment of outgoing force. All that tends to keep the earth settled and quiet, on the other hand, spread out flat on the surface where least liable to upset, so to speak, is Yin, the horizontal element. All Chinese art must find balance, and because of its three-dimensional use of varied objects, the garden is considered a particularly sensitive expression of the artist's effort.

The designer of Chinese gardens moves slowly, and no wonder. A pillared corridor, a plum tree, even a single bamboo sprout is enough to throw the intangible weight of Yang or Yin one way or the other, overturning balance. And this would cause more unpleasant disturbance to the fastidious Chinese than a pest of dandelions in the grass of a careful gardener at home.

GARDEN SPLENDOR

Restraint amounting to emptiness is a characteristic of Chinese gardens, the traveler decides. Then hundreds of miles from Peking he comes upon such exotic crowded garden opulence as he will not see again.

Hien T'ung Ssu is a monastery in the W'u T'ai Shan,

terracing up a hill. Intricate stairways and platforms mount over Kang H'si turquoise roofs; green and purple walls, laced brick balustrades, gold pagodas in shapes to gladden modern sculptors; pedestals and handrails of carved white marble; heaps of plants in bright porcelain tubs—all crowd up toward a *tempietto* covered with sheets of carved gold, rising like a proud bantam cook between flanking Tibetan palaces. Back of it all, a fierce blue sky.

No European grandeur, no lapis and malachite in Leningrad's Winter Palace conveys the spirit of mad riches and imperial extravagance like these teeming gorgeous baubles flung around Buddha's toy. Children playing hide-and-seek would count it fairyland. And, indeed, it calls up spirits who unveil a new facet of the puzzling jewel, forever balancing on the snout of the tantalizing Chinese dragon.

DESIGN GROWTH IN CHINA

After seeing everything from Newport mansions to whole cities torn down just to make room for the latest novelty, it is soothing to feel the timelessness of a design idea in a less volatile civilization. Not that the temples and gardens in China are static by any means; alterations made through the centuries are plain to see. They continue today, though the tempo is so slow that the American doubts it now and again. Yet the essential program holds; the original idea lives and is respected. Modifications and additions are witness of both permanence and growth.

Continuity of development through the centuries is like that of our institutions which are started with a good policy and maintained by an ever-living board of trustees. It is not conceivable that any one individual designer could have put together all the elements of which the best Chinese landscape compositions are made. They are rather the residue of many minds at intervals, all devoted to the fruitful solution of one continuing problem. And they are as harmonious as spring leaves on an old tree.

The undying idea together with willing compromise help each other. The man who planted the lace bark pine on the Ordination Terrace at J'ai T'ai Ssu hundreds of years ago could not control the exquisite distribution of its branches nor the precision of their relation to roof lines and walls, many if not all of which were built later. The etching of spruces against mountain and sky at Chen Hai Ssu needed planting, clearing and trimming from one generation to another before it could be what we see today. If war has destroyed it, as report says, trees will grow again, and they will be tended. Details may change, but the picture will revive as could be only in China where landscape design lives and grows as man and nature grow.

After the first skeleton idea is established, it may be long before culmination. Progress may be interrupted. A couple of days' ride from Tai Yuan Fu they are working hard on a terrace for giants which was begun, we were told, A.D. 1175. Sad to say, the part that was done while Columbus was hunting for it on the other side of the world, has slipped down the mountain without anybody caring much. Evidently they intended to finish the far end before considering repairs. Yet the idea of the design persists. In some reincarnation, Columbus will see it yet, complete.

Under ordinary circumstances changes in landscape design are due almost exclusively to accretion. The court is built and lived in. In due course a tree is planted to ward off the sun, after consultation with breeze and clouds. Along comes someone who sighs for a sacred rock. He is satisfied. For an anniversary a bronze cauldron is cast with appropriate inscriptions. After endless calculation a sundial is carved and installed. Elimination is unthinkable under these conditions. Now and again something disintegrates, like Columbus' wall or, more likely, a terra cotta tub. A branch or two are cut to improve the pattern of the foliage. Meantime life goes on and does not forget the design idea with which the landscape was first propitiated with incense and ceremony.

ROBERT ZION
(b. 1921)

*Robert Zion, whose landscape architectural practice is
international in scope, has much in common with Thomas
Church, who practiced almost exclusively in California. Both
of these leaders in the profession have based their
extraordinarily sensitive landscape designs on a thorough
knowledge of the technical aspects of their craft. Zion's
approach to designing with trees emphasizes their value in
the urban landscape.*

Trees for Architecture and the Landscape

Designing with Trees—an Approach

There are no hard and fast rules of design in any medium—merely a personal approach which, if valid and combined with a mastery of technical aspects, can lead to good design. Presented here is a series of observations which comprise the author's personal approach to planting trees.

The Tree in Design

Landscape architecture is the forming and interrelating of countless compositions in space intended to be walked through, run through, driven through, played in, sat in, and freely used in general. These spaces are enriched by the landscape architect from a palette of design elements, of which the tree is only one, although certainly the most interesting one.

Trees can be considered essential to a design, rather than an embellishment, only when they are massed to form the wall of a space. This architectonic use of trees was characteristic of the gardens of Le Notre and his followers in eighteenth century France, where trees were pleached and pollarded to form walls and canopies of green for vast outdoor rooms. . . .

Source: New York: Reinhold, 1968.

SKILLS OF THE LANDSCAPE DESIGNER

A thorough knowledge of arboriculture is an absolute essential to the successful use of trees in landscape design—about this there can be no compromise. Such knowledge must extend far beyond identification of genus or species, or familiarity with sources of supply; it must be a knowledge based on experience with every aspect of the tree—its growth habit, soil preference, reaction to transplanting and pruning; its hardiness to climatic extremes, resistance against or susceptibility to diseases or fungus or insect pests; its moisture requirements; its life expectancy; sunlight or shade requirements, tolerance of salt spray, carbon monoxide, or other hazards, natural or of man's making; and finally a knowledge of the company it keeps, more technically termed ecology—those plants with which it is at home in nature, which have similar preferences of cultivation and with which it looks most natural.

Knowledge of the medium in which one works is clearly an essential to success in any field. In landscape architecture it is not a simple matter acquired automatically with a college degree; it can be gained only by working with trees, by having planted and transplanted and cultivated them, by constantly observing them, and mentally recording observations of their reactions. Only with such knowledge can trees be used properly in landscape design.

A sensual imagination, the ability to project one's self into a design and to understand how it "feels" to walk this way or that in a space which exists at first only on paper, this is perhaps the most important attribute of a creative landscape architect.

A skillful designer must also have a *highly developed visual imagination,* an ability to see each tree in its maturity, to see its changing colors in each season and its changing form over the years. Among designers today there seems to be an emphasis of the visual over the sensual, and it is in this aspect that the designs of different landscape architects differ most radically. It is the author's opinion that, although the visual aspect must be pleasing, no landscape can claim true success if it is not refreshing to be *in*. The quality of design has become increasingly important today. With the rapid disappearance of open space it is extravagant merely to create pretty pictures. Outdoor space must perform an important function, especially in our cities—it must refresh the soul.

CONSTANT BUT PREDICTABLE CHANGE

Trees change constantly in shape, color, and size, but they are not mercurial. All changes can be anticipated by the designer who knows and understands trees. The fall foliage color of each variety is predictable and varies only in intensity from year to year. General conformation varies only in minor degree among different specimens of the same variety. Only a design that anticipates these changes of color and form and capitalizes on them can be truly successful, for such a design elicits the maximum contribution from each tree.

FOUR-DIMENSIONAL DESIGN

This element of change means that for the landscape architect a design is not completed when his plans have been executed. The completion of a planting is only the beginning of a process in which time in combination with the natural phenomenon of growth carries the design forward. A capable designer will anticipate the rate and amount of growth to be expected of the species he has used in his design, thereby ensuring proper spacing of the trees in maturity in relation to buildings and to each other. Designers unfamiliar with trees ignore future development, considering only the immediate effect. Their designs have often been acclaimed and photographed by admirers, who return after leaf-fall to see a space disintegrate because trees have been used as two-dimensional building material instead of living growing objects that must be considered in *time* as well as *space*.

APPROPRIATE DESIGN

Since landscape architectural design is most often created in relation to enframing buildings, it must relate itself closely in quality to the surrounding architecture. It must be *appropriate:* appropriate in choice of plant materials and in degree of enrichment, appropriate color in and vitality to the buildings of which it is a part, and appropriate to the use for which it has been designed.

Perhaps appropriate design is the landscape architect's greatest challenge, for in accomplishing this he must often restrain his efforts to the level of the created architecture and to the general environment. A landscape development that by its very excellence calls attention to itself can never be an integral part of a composition and cannot therefore be considered successful. Appropriateness can be attained only by a thorough and perceptive study of the architecture that enframes the space, the materials used, the uses to which the structure and spaces are to be put, the people who will be using the space, the design and materials used in neighboring projects in the area, and similar related items.

The concept of appropriateness of design applies also to the selection of tree species. Trees used in a design should be consistent with those existing on the site and with neighboring plantings. Beautiful and wondrous as trees are, they can often be inappropriate in shape, size, or intensity of color for a specific use. Properly selected and placed, they can augment the visual and sensual aspects of a space; inappropriately used, they can destroy the space itself.

DOMINANT TREE

To insure unity in a planting design it is wise to select one tree species to be used in greater quantity than any other and to be placed in all principal spaces. Such a dominant tree will, by the repetition of its form, color, and texture, lend continuity to the design.

Similar emphasis-by-repetition of smaller trees—particularly flowering species—is especially useful in effecting recall from one area to another.

MASS PLANTING

Boldness in designing with trees as with other forms of design can seldom fail. Mass plantings of a single variety in close spacing, as in a grove . . . , is highly effective. This is particularly true in the use of flowering trees.

LIMITED PLANT LIST

As in architecture, a restful elegance can be achieved in planting by simplicity of detail and material. The use of only a few tree species and varieties closely related by texture, form, and color will lend this quality to a design. Such restraint in the use of trees is especially important in close proximity to buildings to avoid distracting from the architecture.

ARCHITECTURAL TREES

Certain species have a regularity of form that is retained without pruning. Such regularity of form lends itself to regular or geometric spacing as in an avenue or grove where all trees must be matched. For architectural plantings of this kind it is inconsistent to use a tree such as the common honey-locust with its lacy foliage and characteristically non-conforming open crown, or the ginkgo with its irregular, jagged outline. Architectural or ordered plantings call for a density of foliage and branching in order to present a strongly outlined silhouette in winter as well as summer: the little-leaf linden is such a tree; the honey-locust is not. Neither is the ginkgo.

EVERGREEN SKELETON

A planting design that disintegrates in winter when defoliation of deciduous trees takes place is a weak design. Evergreens, properly used, can provide a skeleton that gives year-round structure to outdoor space, contributing color and contrast as well. Evergreen trees are also useful in providing recall from one area to another.

COLOR

Color in the landscape must be massed to be effective. The use of single trees of colorful foliage or blossom creates a restless scene; groups of trees (three or more) of similar color are more effective. Colorful trees also aid in providing recall. A word of caution, however, against too great a variety of unrelated colors and the use of colors that conflict with architecture.

Specimen Tree

The isolated specimen tree of unusual size, shape, color, or texture is an excellent device to emphasize a point in the spatial composition or draw the eye toward or away from some aspect of the architecture. The specimen tree placed in a space of proper proportions should be used as one would use sculpture.

"Dirty" Trees

Every client has some private tree prejudice; there is always some tree considered "dirty." This concept remains an anomaly to the author, for most trees lose their leaves, all flowering trees lose their blossoms, and many shed their bark. But these all have the compensating advantages of seasonal change, handsome trunks, etc. It is true that most fast-growing trees have brittle wood which is often broken in storms, but these trees also have the distinct advantage of rapid growth and immediate effect at less cost than other varieties.

Native Trees

It is always wise to plant species native to the site if they adequately fulfill the design requirements, for these species have already proved themselves hardy in the soil and climatic conditions of the area. This will mean fewer maintenance problems in terms of winter protection, summer watering, soil enrichment, and other care.

In any case, whenever possible, trees should be purchased from local sources, since plant material introduced from great distances must struggle with the problem of adjustment to climatic differences in addition to the shock of transplanting.

IMMEDIATE EFFECT

Immediate effect is the term given to a planting which, because of the size of the tree used, presents a mature appearance from the outset. Under most circumstances planning an entire planting for immediate effect is an error, for the owner then has nothing to look forward to. Even those who are most in a hurry should be given the pleasure of watching some trees mature. On commercial projects, however, where the planting assumes a certain advertising value, immediate effect is often an appropriate approach. And even under the most stringent budgetary limitations, it is always desirable to use a few trees of four-inch caliber or more at important locations in the design to relieve the "new look" of a project.

PLANTING FOR THE FUTURE

Planting for the future is seldom done in this country. We have lost the patience necessary to watch small trees mature. Yet the beech groves that we find so enchanting in England today would not exist if this attitude had prevailed there 75 years ago.

College campuses and certainly public buildings with a long life-expectancy should be planted to long-lived varieties such as the beech and white oak which are very slow to mature. These can be used in combination with faster-growing varieties to provide some immediate effect.

TREE ECOLOGY

The designer is wise to respect certain ecological relationships among trees. Trees associated in nature have a more comfortable appearance when used together; they are usually complementary in color and texture, and have similar cultivation requirements. When they are used together maintenance is obviously simpler than when trees with different moisture and soil requirements are grouped.

CARLTON B. LEES
(1924–1989)

As executive director of the Massachusetts Horticultural Society, Carlton Lees influenced many people who were in the beginning primarily interested in plants. He helped them to see how plants make a garden, and in this book, how plants and gardens led to the creation of more public spaces and finally resulted in the beautification of these spaces.

———————

GARDENS, PLANTS
AND MAN

Out of one wintry twig,
One bud
One blossom's worth of warmth
At long last
    RANSTSU (1653–1708)
    HAIKU HARVEST

Gardens are the most complex of the arts, for they deal with the organization of outdoor space within which all other arts are contained or take place. The Villa Lante and George Washington's Mount Vernon were conceived as entities, as two unified spaces inside which are contained buildings, pathways, pools, plants and all other materials and objects which meet man's needs and contribute to his comfort and pleasure. They are places *for* man. Garden is the art of *making a place* as opposed to just letting it happen.

In spite of those who fought for the picturesque, gardens are less related to painting than to architecture. Both architecture and gardens shape space to contain people. A painting is two-dimensional; it is only to be looked at but not entered into. Sculpture is three-dimensional, but until recently it was looked at only from the outside; when you move into the new sculpture, it tends to become architecture.

It is easy when studying gardens to be misled by two-dimensional plans, drawings, engravings and photographs which also emphasize the pictorial. From them it is nearly impossible to gain a sense of the space of the garden, of

Source: Englewood Cliffs, N.J.: A Rutledge Book, Prentice-Hall, Inc., 1970.

height and width and depth. While gardens such as the Villa Lante do have much in them that is pictorial, the primary quality is of organized space.

When James Rose said that being in a garden should be like being inside a piece of hollow sculpture he underlined the fact that the success of a garden depends upon the quality of its enclosed space. In order to understand this concept, it is necessary to become aware of the volume of a garden and recognize our place within that volume. In this sense a garden is roomlike, but its walls, floors and ceilings are much more diversified than those of a room. The floors are lawn, paving, water, flower beds. The walls are hedges, foliage masses, fences, distant views, and the roofs may be arbor, vine, sky or overhanging branches of trees.

But in order to recognize the space itself, it is necessary to ignore, at least momentarily, the details of the confining structures and materials. One can become enveloped in a garden composition just as in the composition of a great interior space. The excitement of being in a great cathedral comes from the shape of the enclosed space, not from the details of the floors, walls and ceilings.

The Abby Aldrich Rockefeller Sculpture Garden of the Museum of Modern Art in New York City is a place made for occupancy by human beings. Although it contains sculpture, the garden itself is also sculpturelike: it is exactly what James Rose must have had in mind. Man can move about within the volume of the garden and find it an exciting and dignifying experience. This garden is a *made place,* a delightful, comfortable and wonderful place. It is a bridge between the nearly completely artificial neighborhood and the natural world. It is also an extremely successful demonstration of how outdoor space can become important in terms of human experience because of the direct action of man.

Another outgrowth of our approach to gardens as mere

pictures has resulted in gardens having been hung on the wall, in a sense, and relegated to the decorative unnecessary. As a nation we have never considered gardens necessary. Yet Professor George E. Hutchinson, an ecologist at Yale, tells us that America is in trouble because "people can't sit in gardens, watch birds around them. . . ." Professor Hutchinson is one of many concerned about the excesses of mankind. He has said that he thinks we will survive but warns, " . . . the cost to the satisfactions of life will be enormous. There is already a reaction to overcrowding in the cities—riots. . . . We need more research not only on the minimal needs of people in cities but also on the optimal needs."

The most obvious is often least seen. While we have been building bigger and faster and more automated cars, washing machines and can openers we have forgotten that human life is something that requires quality as well as quantity. The hardness of asphalt, concrete and steel is becoming increasingly oppressive. We are just beginning to learn that the need to sit under trees and watch birds is important for our mental and physical well-being. Science is discovering new relationships between living foliage and clean air. John Ruskin wrote, "I have never heard of a piece of land which would let well as a building lease remaining unlet because it was a flowery place. . . ." (*Modern Painters,* George Allen, Sunnyside, Orpington, Kent, 1878).

If there is to be a tomorrow in which people can live as dignified human beings, there will have to be more land remaining unlet for "flowery pieces." Wilderness and national parks are important but so, too, are the city, the suburb and that awful no-man's-land in between which has been called the "Slurb." If the landscape is bad, it is because man has made it so. He can preserve a place, he can make a place—or he can destroy a place.

In the final analysis it is every man who makes the difference. Every man at some point in his life should plant a bean so he will come to understand that it is necessary to his sustenance. He should plant a tree to learn that it is necessary to his comfort, and he should plant a rose to learn something of grace.

Men makes places, but places also make men.

LESTER HAWKINS
(1915–1985)

Western Hills nursery in Occidental, California, has achieved legendary status because of the efforts of Lester Hawkins and his partner, Marshall Olbrich. Their garden and nursery became a mecca for plant lovers during the '80s because of the enthusiasm, knowledge, and hard work that these men brought to gardening. Specifically American in his well-considered, practical point of view, Hawkins helped gardeners adapt plants and ideas from around the world to the landscape and architecture of this country.

———————

THE PACIFIC
HORTICULTURE BOOK OF
WESTERN GARDENING

Planting the Plantsman's Garden

For all serious gardeners 1983 was a significant centennial, for it was in November 1883 that William Robinson's *The English Flower Garden* was published. This event was important not only for the English, but for gardeners everywhere who enjoy and want to grow a wide range of plants.

It is difficult to pinpoint revolutions in taste. Already, by 1883, Great Britain had seen a tremendous influx of plants from all over the world, and there were many gardens that were also sizable collections. However, Robinson's great work was at once a strongly worded manifesto and an enthusiastic spelling out of the possibilities of the plantsman's garden. It describes in considerable detail almost everything we need to know to plant at least one kind of informal and graceful garden in which a diversity of plants could be made to lie down in harmony.

Robinson's title is misleading; he covers not only flowers but every conceivable aspect of the gardener's art: hedges, trees, evergreen shrubs, even garden structures, rock gardens, and ponds. So complete is this remarkable book that the works of virtually all subsequent garden authors, from Gertrude Jekyll to Frances Perry and Graham Stuart Tho-

Source: Boston: David R. Godine in association with the Pacific Horticultural Foundation, 1990. Edited by George Waters and Nora Harlow.

mas, can be thought of as so many marginal notes to it. Thirty-six years before the appearance of Farrer's *English Rock Garden,* Robinson was urging a more naturalistic laying of rock and deep and gritty drainage for a truly successful alpine garden. Here, twenty-nine years before Miss Jekyll's *Colour Schemes for the Garden,* were many of the ideas for perennial borders that she carried out and expanded. Most astonishing, perhaps, are Robinson's list of plants for various purposes. A hundred years later I am hard put to think of a vine, a fragrant plant, or a good perennial that he did not mention at least by genus.

Robinson and Jekyll both hated formality and were fond of describing their plantings as "natural" or as similar to "painting pictures." I don't think these authors were aware how odd their choice of words was. Most often, the plant combinations they mentioned were unlike anything found in nature; even as "pictures," there is nothing on earth they could be said to represent. By a curious inversion, Robinson makes the extraordinary claim that if English gardens were as well planted as he would like them to be, artists would prefer them to nature as subject matter.

The idea of nature is obviously large and many-faceted. It has been variously defined, and at different times differing choices among its many faces have been emphasized. Most often words like "natural" are the rallying cries of those in revolt against what they see as the excesses of artifice and the stilted fashions that threaten to gain a stranglehold on the morals or tastes of a civilization. We can, therefore, best discover what these authors meant not by asking for definitions, but by examining what they were rebelling against and how they proposed to remedy it.

VICTORIAN ARTIFICE

In mid-Victorian times, before Robinson's influence began to be felt and after the late-eighteenth-century fashion of landscape gardening, there was a long period of return to formality. Parterres, hedges, fountains, bedding-out schemes, long, straight avenues, and abundant terracing were the order of the day. Judging from all the descriptions, it was deplorable, lacking as it did the grandeur of French formal gardens and the grace and intricacy of their Italian counterparts. There were statues, but they were awful statues; fountains, but they were ugly; pergolas and gazebos, but they were ungainly. In the growing prosperity of the British Empire, most of these things were bought by the newly prosperous to impress rather than to charm. Robinson's descriptions of all this are exasperated; he hated it so. This is, in a way, unfortunate, because it made him an uneven and crotchety writer. To discover his remarkable world, we must fight again a battle that has long since been won, and it is difficult to discern the peaceful beauty he expounded through the turmoil and dust of his struggle.

Robinson particularly hated excess terraces, which he compares to railway embankments and to fortifications "made by Uncle Toby and an army of Corporal Tims." He writes:

> The landscape gardener, too often led by custom, falls in with the notion that every house, no matter what its position, should be fortified by terraces and he busies himself forming them even on level ground, and large sums are spent on fountains, vases, statues, ballustrades, useless walls, and stucco work out of place.

The plantings are, if anything, worse:

On top of all this formality of design of our day were grafted the most formal and inartistic ways of arranging flowers that ever came into the head of man. . . . Bedding out, or marshalling the flowers in stiff lines and geometrical patterns, is entirely a thing of our precious time and 'carpet' gardening is simply a further remove in ugliness.

Much of this folly, Robinson says—and this I think is still true today—comes from giving architects too much power and from the "too facile labors of the drawing board artist." It would be difficult to exaggerate the depth of his feelings on this score.

Any pupil in an architect's office will get out a drawing for the kind of garden we see everywhere. . . . It is the difference between life and death we have to think of, and never to the end of time shall we get the garden beautiful formed or planted save by men who know something of the earth and its flowers, shrubs, and trees.

In Robinson's mind, the natural was a clear and beckoning goal that rose above all considerations of style, a word he hated and usually put in quotes. Criticizing a garden writer who talks about style, he says:

What is the result to anybody who looks from words to things? That there are two styles; the one strait-laced, mechanical, with much wall and stone, with fountains and sculpture; the other the natural, which, once free of the house, accepts the ground lines of the earth herself as the best and gets plant beauty from the flowers and trees arranged in picturesque ways.

And there we have it; the common conceit that one has risen above all fashion and all history into the light of the truth.

The natural and the picturesque are not the geometrical, the architectural, and the formal. What, then, are they? Robinson's efforts at definition are vague, but we can infer much from his descriptions of his favorite garden projects, his flower borders, shady walks, rock arrangements, and bog gardens; from his notes on the placement of trees and shrubs; and from his ideas of light and shade and the circulation of air in the garden.

THE ROBINSON IDEAL

Central to his thinking is the use of an abundance of plants; a feature of nature is said to be variety, and "the question is, how the garden lover is to enjoy as many of these treasures as his conditions allow of." Apart from the woods where there is natural leaf mold, there is no bare ground, and in all the descriptions there is a feeling of luxuriance, sometimes even a riot of foliage, flowers, and plant forms.

Robinson quotes with approval the artist and gardener, Frank Miles, who writes:

> Well, supposing the back of the border filled with delphiniums, phloxes and roses, pegged down, and other summer and autumn blooming plants . . . I should carpet the ground at the back with spring blooming flowers, so that when the roses are bare and the delphiniums and phloxes have not pushed above ground, the border should even then be a blaze of beauty. Crocuses, snowdrops, aconites, and primroses are quite enough for that purpose. The whole space under the roses I should cover with the

common wood anemone and the golden wood anemone, and early cyclamens and the earliest dwarf daffodils. And among the roses and paeonies and other medium-sized shrubs I would put all the taller lilies, such as require continual shade on their roots; and such as pardalinum and the Californian lilies generally, the Japanese, Chinese and finer American lilies. Now we come to the front of the border, and here I would have combinations, such as the great St. Bruno's lily and the delicate hybrid columbines, primroses planted over hardy gladioli . . . carnations and daffodils planted so that the carnations form a blaze of blue-green for the delicate creams and oranges of the daffodils. . . .

The picture gradually unfolds: densely planted borders, vines on pergolas and walls (and sometimes on trees and shrubs as well), rock and dry-wall gardens chock full of plants that thrive there, ponds edged with reeds, water irises, cannas, and much more. As we walk into the woods, the paths are bordered at first with closely planted sun-loving plants, then those that like the shelter and frost protection of dappled shade, and finally to the genuine shade lovers. Some tropical plants are bedded out—bananas, tender palms, and philodendrons.

Any feeling of congestion is relieved by broad, rolling lawns, and all is contrived to fit into its setting with as little alteration of grade as possible. Above all, there is geometry only near the house.

We have, in short, what the world now knows as the English garden. In England, there has been no real revolution in taste since the appearance of *The English Flower Garden*. Writers such as Christopher Lloyd, Margery Fish, and Beth Chatto have laid more emphasis on selectivity, refinement, and unity of effect, but they all stress variety in planting—though none would urge, as Robinson did, that the gardener plant "as many of these treasures as his conditions allow of."

Alas, we cannot say that William Robinson superseded all styles and found his way to the ultimate truth of the natural mode. He is, we must say it, very *fin de siècle,* or late Victorian in his opulence. Natural would be a strange term to apply to the garden feature for which he and Gertrude Jekyll are most famous: the long, straight, double flower border backed on both sides with hedges. Or to what Robinson approvingly called "one of the brightest colored beds I have ever seen," consisting of *Sedum acre* 'Elegans', creamy white; *Sedum glaucum,* gray; *Herniaria glabra,* green; *Aptenia cordifolia* 'Variegatum' (*Mesembryanthemum cordifolium*), light yellow; bright orange and scarlet alternatheras; the central plants being *Grevillea robusta* and variegated abutilons. Clearly, for all his protestations, Robinson was a product of his times.

I am sometimes appalled by Robinson, but I far more often agree with him and the feeling of communion and rapport runs deep. I agree that plantings should be graceful, well-rounded, and informal, and that they should charm rather than impress. I agree that plans on paper drawn up in offices do not make gardens. And I too like to use a wide variety of plants, although perhaps not with quite the same abandon. Even before I read *The English Flower Garden,* Robinson's world in many ways was mine as well. In our changed circumstances, I hope I have kept something of his spirit if little of his letter in the following observations and suggestions of my own for creating effective plantings.

First, however, I should like briefly to compare the "natural" plantings of Robinson, Jekyll, and their disciples with those other "natural" plantings of the great landscape gardeners a hundred years previously. On the one hand we have a crowded canvas bright with colored foliage and flowers; on the other there is quiet, uneventful serenity. But that is not all; there is also an extreme difference in scale. Gertrude Jekyll spent her life earnestly tending a ten-acre plot. "Capability" Brown had hundreds, sometimes thousands, of acres at his disposal, and, once planted, they were never to be dug again.

The differences are there for all to see at Stourhead, in Wiltshire, where the followers of Robinson and Jekyll have planted colored foliage trees and flowering shrubs in a sparse and serene eighteenth-century landscape. There are many, even today, who find these additions excrescences that should be removed. To Brown, the "natural" was a landscape stretching as far as the eye could see, similar to one that might be found in some privileged place undisturbed by man. To Jekyll and Robinson it was bits and pieces of nature—the edge of a pond, the crowded verge of a copse, or a riot of wildflowers—to be imported, laboriously cultivated, and used to grace a well-trodden path. There are many other differences, of course. We also have to consider such factors as the great plant introductions into England in the nineteenth century, the late-eighteenth-century taste for classical simplicity, and the Victorian taste for opulence. Nevertheless, it is plain that nature is an alluring but varied guide, and now, a hundred years later still, we shall try again to capture the natural, and on plots that have become even smaller.

MIXED PLANTINGS

Perhaps the most useful planting for small gardens and one that can be extraordinarily handsome almost anywhere is a border that mixes, more or less deliberately, the basic categories of plants—basic, that is, in the gardening sense. Perennials, shrubs, bulbs, and grasses can be combined in ways reminiscent of memorable scenes in nature and capable of providing interest the year round. I remember in Greece in late spring, on the island of Evia, a mixture that could well be copied just as it was. In the middle ground were euphorbias, lavenders, and campanulas (some of which were twining through the lavenders). These were backed by brooms and rock roses with low meadow annuals and bulbs—mostly anemones—in the foreground. For a garden we might want to extend the flowering season by adding later-flowering bulbs—*Allium christophii* (*A. albopilosum*) and *A. pulchellum*, perhaps—and some summer- and fall-flowering low perennial—origanums undoubtedly, and helichrysums.

Along a path at Knightshayes Court in the west of England there is a sizable drift of white martagon lilies with, in the foreground, a silvery and blue grass interplanted with dwarf lavenders. This planting has the merit of great simplicity. The totality was a memorable picture (as Gertrude Jekyll would say), but it also was effective in displaying the individual beauty of each of these plants.

One obvious advantage of the mixed border is that it is the best possible home for bulbs, which are often difficult to place in the perennial border and by themselves leave bare ground for considerable periods. In another English garden *Allium rosenbachianum* was in flower among *Stachys macrantha*, with its deep rose panicles, both in front of a shell-pink dwarf rose. Without detracting from the whole effect, it is possible in such a planting to leave bits of bare ground for bulbs such as nerines, after carefully calculating whether the neighbors on all sides will be compatible at flowering time.

Innumerable plants are available for the mixed border, but it is important to keep them all more or less within the same general scale (a useful cue one can take from nature).

By scale I do not mean only size; it is not always a thing you can measure, but it is something we can generally agree on. A mullein, for example, may shoot skyward out of a bed of thistles by the roadside. The mullein has larger leaves, greater height, and a thicker stem than the thistle, but both are obviously lush, lowland plants, and neither looks out of scale. If, on the other hand, we make the mistake of planting a diminutive dianthus (which belongs in the alpine garden) with artemisias and lavenders a foot or more high, the dianthus not only will eventually be overrun, it will look out of place from the start. I have found that a good way to judge scale is to allow one or preferably two of the plants I intend to use to stand as a measure against which I judge the others—*Origanum hybridum* and *Salvia officinalis,* for example, or *Alchemilla vulgaris* and *Geranium macrorrhizum.*

There are many shrubs that can be used with plants of the stature of a medium-sized dianthus for pathside plantings. Among my favorites are the elegant *Arctostaphylos nummularia* 'Anchor Bay', many hebes of the size of *Hebe menziesii,* and *Rhododendron racemosum,* one of the best small rhododendrons for general planting in the garden. Many barberries are possibilities, including *Berberis calliantha,* with its graceful hanging flowers and the dwarf red-leaved *B. thunbergii* 'Atropurpurea'. Dwarf brooms are not only showy in flower but offer a variety of picturesque evergreen forms for year-round effect. And most of the well-known deciduous flowering shrubs have dwarf species or forms—*Syringa patula* (*S. palibiniana*), a dwarf *Viburnum plicatum* 'Mariesii', or *Philadelphus × purpureomaculatus* 'Nuage Rose', to name a few.

Candidates for the herbaceous parts of our pathside can often be found among those plants that are beautiful, but too large or too rampant for the rock garden, which should be reserved for diminutive gems from the high mountains. Such plants are *Omphalodes cappadocica, Gypsophila repens* 'Rosea', *Lithodora diffusa* 'Grace Ward' (*Lithospermum diffusum*), *Helichrysum* 'Moe's Gold' (which blooms in October), and *Diascia cordata.*

Grasses somewhat on the same scale are the Japanese blood grass, *Imperata cylindrica,* the bulbous grass, *Arrhenatherum elatius* 'Variegatum', and *Hakonechloa macra* 'Albo Aurea'. There are also many colorful sedges, particularly from the New Zealand Alps. All of these plants are ideal in size for the average garden path, for mixed plantings in front of larger shrubs, in front of small trees on the sunny side, or for islands in lawns that do not obtrude far above the grass.

One way to start thinking about such a planting is to begin with two plants that are extraordinarily handsome together—*Trachelium caeruleum* and the pink stokesia, for example—and gradually add plants that will further enhance the effect, such as *Aster × frikartii* 'Mönch', the beautiful deep red grass, *Pennisetum setaceum* 'Cupreum', *Picea glauca* 'Montgomery', and *Allium pulchellum.* Another way is to choose a geographical theme, a mixed planting of Mediterranean, for example, or of California natives.

The mixed planting is ideal for displaying plant collections, provided the plants are of a size to be accommodated. A collection of dwarf grasses or sempervivums, for example, can be planted along a curving path together with bulbs, small perennials, and alpines of the right size in a way that gives a natural touch without detracting from the enthusiast's interest in the plants themselves.

Here I have been thinking of more or less ordinary pathside plantings, since I agree with Robinson and Jekyll that all spaces in the garden should be utilized. When I see gardens that are primarily roses, perhaps, or rhododendrons, and the paths are either not planted or given over to a dull ground cover, I always wonder at the lost opportunities. It is true that many people see only plants and not gardens, but I have always considered this a curable deficiency.

Many variants of the mixed planting format are possible—those of larger or smaller scale than the above, for example, depending upon the plants to be used and whether delicacy or boldness is the aim.

BIBLIOGRAPHY

Adams, William Howard, ed. *The Eye of Thomas Jefferson.* Washington, D.C.: National Gallery of Art, 1976.

Anderson, Dorothy May. *Women, Design and The Cambridge School.* Lafayette, IN: PDA Publishers Corp., 1980.

Arnold, Henry F. *Trees in Urban Design.* New York: Van Nostrand Reinhold Co., 1980.

Blanchan, Neltje. *The American Flower Garden.* New York: Doubleday, Page and Co., 1909.

Bye, A. E. *Art into Landscape, Landscape into Art.* Mesa, AZ: PDA Publishers Corporation, 1983.

Cautley, Marjorie Sewell. *Garden Design: The Principles of Abstract Design as Applied to Landscape Composition.* New York: Dodd, Mead and Company, 1935.

Church, Thomas D. *Gardens Are for People.* New York: Reinhold Publishing Corporation, 1955.

Bibliography

Coffin, Marian Cruger. *Trees and Shrubs for Landscape Effects.* New York: Charles Scribner's Sons, 1951.

Cornell, Ralph D. *Conspicuous California Plants.* Los Angeles: The Plantin Press, 1938.

Dean, Ruth. *The Livable House: Its Garden.* New York: Moffat Yard & Co., 1917.

Downing, Andrew Jackson. *A Treatise on the Theory and Practice of Landscape Gardening Adapted to North America. . . .* New York: A. O. Moore and Co., 1859.

Earle, Alice Morse. *Old-Time Gardens.* New York: Macmillan Co., 1901.

Eckbo, Garrett. *Landscape for Living.* New York: Duell, Sloan and Pearce, 1950.

Eliot, Charles. *Report of the Board of Metropolitan Park Commissioners,* Boston: 1893.

Ely, Helena Rutherfurd, *A Woman's Hardy Garden.* New York: The Macmillan Co., 1915.

Farrand, Beatrix. *Beatrix Farrand's Plant Book for Dumbarton Oaks.* Edited by Diane Kostial McGuire. Washington D.C.: Dumbarton Oaks, 1980.

Fessenden, Thomas G. *The New American Garden.* Boston: Otis, Broaders, 1854.

Forestier, J. C. M. *Gardens: A Notebook of Plans and Sketches.* New York: Scribner's, 1928.

Fox, Helen Morganthau. *Patio Gardens.* New York: Macmillan, 1925.

Halprin, Lawrence. *Cities.* New York: Reinhold Book Corporation, 1963.

Hawkins, Lester. "Planting the Plantsman's Garden." In *The Pacific Horticulture Book of Western Gardening.* Boston: David R. Godine, 1990.

Hubbard, Henry Vincent, and Theodora Kimball. *An Introduction to the Study of Landscape Design.* New York: 1917.

Jay, Mary Rutherfurd. *The Garden Handbook.* New York: Harper, 1931.

Jefferson, Thomas. *Thomas Jefferson's Garden Book 1766–1824.* Philadelphia: The American Philosophical Society, 1944.

Jensen, Jens. *Siftings.* Chicago: Ralph Fletcher Seymour, 1930.

Bibliography

Kalfus, Melvin. *Frederick Law Olmsted: The Passion of a Public Artist.* New York: New York University Press, 1990.

Lees, Carlton B. *Gardens, Plants and Man.* New Jersey: Prentice-Hall, 1970.

Leighton, Ann. *American Gardens in the Eighteenth Century.* Boston: Houghton Mifflin Co., 1976.

————. *American Gardens of the Nineteenth Century: For Comfort and Affluence.* Amherst: University of Massachusetts Press, 1987.

————. "For Meate or Medicine." In *Early American Gardens.* Boston: Houghton Mifflin Co., 1970.

Lockwood, Alice G. B., ed. *Gardens of Colony and State: Gardens and Gardeners of the American Colonies and of the Republic before 1840.* New York: Scribners, 1931–34.

Lounsberry, Alice. *Gardens Near the Sea.* New York: Frederick A. Stokes Co., 1910.

Maynard, Samuel Taylor. *Landscape Gardening as Applied to Home Decoration.* New York: John Wiley and Sons, 1899.

McGuire, Diane Kostial. *Gardens of America: Three Centuries of Landscape Design.* Charlottesville, VA: Thomasson-Grant, 1989.

————, ed. *Beatrix Jones Farrand Fifty Years of American Landscape Architecture.* Washington, D.C.: Dumbarton Oaks, 1982.

McHarg, Ian L. *Design with Nature.* New York: The Natural History Press, 1969.

McLaren, John. *Gardening in California: Landscape and Flower.* San Francisco: A. M. Robertson, 1900.

Meehan, Thomas. *The American Handbook of Ornamental Trees.* Philadelphia: Lippincott, Grambo & Co., 1853.

Newton, Norman T. *Design on the Land.* Cambridge, MA: Harvard University Press, 1971.

Nichols, Rose Standish. *Spanish and Portuguese Gardens.* Boston: Houghton Mifflin Co., 1924.

Olmsted, Frederick Law. *Walks and Talks of an American Farmer in England.* New York: Rikei, Thorne and Co., 1854.

Padilla, Victoria. *Southern California Gardens: An Illustrated History.* Berkeley: University of California Press, 1961.

Pennsylvania Horticultural Society, *From Seed to Flower, Philadelphia 1681–1876.* Philadelphia: Pennsylvania Horticultural Society, 1976.

Platt, Charles. *Italian Gardens.* New York: Harper and Brothers, 1894.

Rehman, Elsa. *Garden-Making.* Boston: Houghton Mifflin Co., 1926.

Rose, James. *Modern American Gardens Designed by James Rose.* New York: Reinhold, 1967.

Scott, Frank J. *The Art of Beautifying Suburban Home Grounds of Small Extent.* New York: 1870.

Shinn, Charles H. *Pacific Rural Handbook.* San Francisco: Dewey and Co., 1879.

Smith, Alice Upham. *Trees in a Winter Landscape.* New York: Holt, Rinehart and Winston, 1969.

Smithson, Robert. *The Writings of Robert Smithson: Essays with Illustrations.* Edited by Nancy Holt. New York: New York University Press, 1979.

Solomon, Barbara Stauffacher. *Green Architecture and the Agrarian Garden.* New York: Rizzoli International Publications, Inc., 1988.

Steele, Fletcher. *Gardens and People.* New York: Houghton Mifflin Co., 1964.

Stilgoe, John. *Common Landscape of America: 1580 to 1845.* New Haven, CT: Yale University Press, 1982.

Tahn, Grace. *Old-Fashioned Gardening, A History and a Reconstruction.* New York: McBride, Nast & Co., 1913.

Tatum, George B., and Elisabeth B. MacDougall, eds. *Prophet with Honor: The Career of Andrew Jackson Downing, 1815–1852.* Washington, D.C.: Dumbarton Oaks, 1989.

Thaxter, Celia. *An Island Garden.* Boston: Houghton Mifflin Co., 1894.

Wharton, Edith. *Italian Villas and their Gardens.* New York: The Century Co., 1905.

Wilder, Louise Beebe. *The Garden in Color.* New York: Macmillan, 1937.

———. *Pleasures and Problems of a Rock Garden.* New York: Doubleday, Doran & Co., Inc., 1928.

Yoch, James J. *Landscaping the American Dream: The Gardens and Film Sets of Florence Yoch, 1890–1972.* New York: Harry M. Abrams/ Saga Press, 1989.

Zion, Robert. *Trees for Architecture and the Landscape.* New York: Reinhold, 1968.

INDEX

❧

Abby Aldrich Rockefeller Sculpture Garden, 227
Abutilons, 237
Acacia, 56, 63
Achillea, 180
Aconite, 152
Actinidia, 121
Adams, John, 55
Adams, John Quincy, 55
Ageratum, 123
Ailanthus, 30
Alchemilla vulgaris, 240
Alder, 107
Allium albopilosum, 239; *A. christophii*, 239; *A. pulchellum*, 239, 241; *A. rosenbachianum*, 239
Alpine gardens, 72, 232, 240
Alternathera, 237
Althea, 37, 55, 99, 108
Alyssum, 120, 168
American Flower Garden, The (Blanchan), 66, 67–79
Anchusa myosotidiflora, 116
Andromeda, 142, 198
Anemone, 116, 122, 239
Antigravity materials, plants as, 155–59; and arrangement, 177–79; and color, 163–73; and costs, 173–74; and enclosure, 182–83; and form, 159–61; and native vs. foreign plants, 174–77; and shelter, 183–90; and surfacing, 179–82; and texture, 161–63
Aptenia cordifolia, 237

Aquilegia, 95. *See also* Columbine
Arabis, 151
Arborvitae, 106, 108, 111, 138, 147
Architecture: American, 75–76; style of, and style of garden, 76–77, 80, 90
Arctostaphylos nummularia, 240; *A. uva-ursi*, 200. *See also* Bearberry
Arrhenatherum elatius, 241
Arrow-wood, 105, 107
Artemisia, 48, 240
Ash, 30, 40, 54, 141, 198
Asters, 94, 96, 113, 117, 120, 122, 138, 140
Aster × *frikartii*, 241
Avocado, 164
Azalea, 59, 140, 193, 194, 198, 200
Azalea amoena, 193; *A. hinodegiri*, 193; *A. hinomayo*, 193; *A. macrantha*, 193

Bachelor's buttons, 47
Bacon, Lord, 58, 77
Balsam, 37, 94
Bamboo, 63, 64, 207
Banyan tree, 156
Barberry, 55, 79, 100, 105, 108, 111, 198, 240. *See also Berberis*
Barragan, Luis, 154
Bartram, John, 28
Bayberry, 45, 79, 108, 200
Bearberry, 200. *See also Arctostaphylos*

Index